PROFESSIONAL DEVELOPMENT

Esther A. Meacham
and Mabel M. Sarbaugh

The Ohio State University

Advocate Publishing Group
Box 351, Reynoldsburg, Ohio 43068

ISBN: 0-89894-022-2

Cover design by Gregory Opt
Typesetting by Avatar Media Associates

10   9   8   7   6   5   4   3   2

Printed in the United States of America

PREFACE

Professional Development, originally prepared to supplement the studies of home economics students at The Ohio State University, prepares home economics students and others for some of the pitfalls, and suggests ways to overcome them, as they ready themselves for professional careers. Anyone entering his professional field for the first time or transferring from one area of interest to another will appreciate much of the advice included here.

While the work is intended for use as a workbook for those preparing their professional credentials for the first time, it can continue to serve as a valuable reference.

Although at the present time the majority of home economics students are women, the material included here is geared for a complete audience — both men and women. Articles such as the interview with John Molloy and the account regarding preparing court testimony in the case of a homemaker, may appear to weight the content of the manual to a female orientation. However, the fact that both reflect current trends in our society make them appropriate for consideration by users of the manual.

Appreciation is expressed to the following persons:

— **Delbra Williamson, graduate student in Home Economics Education,** was responsible for the intensive research, writing and putting together of the original manuscript for this book. As the book takes on a new format, appreciation is expressed again to her for her contributions.

— Jeanne Hogarth, a Master's Degree student in the Home Management and Housing Department and teaching associate for the course in which the book is used, for her careful notes and attention to revision.

— All contributors of information who are identified throughout the book.

Mabel Sarbaugh, Professor
and Associate Director,
Faculty, Staff and
Student Services
Esther Meacham, Ph.D.
Professor and Coordinator
of Audiovisual Materials

School of Home Economics
The Ohio State University
Columbus, Ohio

CONTENTS

CHAPTER 1

Standing Up For YOU
(without fear & trembling)

Much has been written in recent years about the benefits of being assertive. Women particularly have benefited from assertion training. No place has this been more apparent than in the job market; for the first time, large numbers of women are seeking professional level positions that involve supervision of others, both male and female. Being assertive is both a part of the interviewing process and a part of effectively performing as an employee once one is hired.

What does it mean to be assertive? How can I tell if I am or am not assertive? Do I always need to be assertive? These are only a few of the questions that may come to your mind as you think of yourself in relation to assertiveness. In considering assertiveness and you, examine the following diagrams:

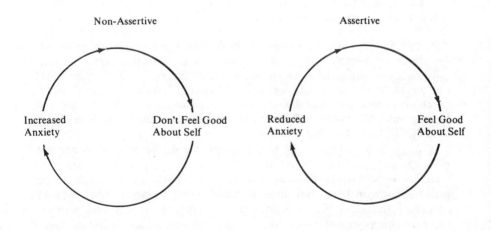

Non-Assertive		Assertive	
Increased Anxiety	Don't Feel Good About Self	Reduced Anxiety	Feel Good About Self
Diagram 1		Diagram 2	

In assertion training, a primary goal is to replace the unassertive (either passive or aggressive) cycle of behavior with an assertive cycle of behavior, thus enabling a person to feel good about himself and reduce the level of anxiety inherent in a particular situation. Becoming assertive involves changing behaviors, both verbally and nonverbally.

DEFINITIONS

Before continuing, it might be helpful to have some working definitions of the terms "passive," "aggressive," and "assertive." Passive and aggressive behaviors are considered to be unassertive although they are very different from one another.

Passive people tend to ignore their own rights and/ or permit others to violate or infringe on their rights. Passive people usually do not say what they want or need; often they are very indirect and self-denying. They let others make decisions for them, feel anxious, and find themselves disappointed. They are often angry but are unwilling to let others know it.

Aggressive people, on the other hand, tend to ignore the rights of others in the process of standing up for what they want. Aggressive people often take advantage of others, put others down, or try to dominate them. Often, they try to tell others how to run their lives. Aggressive people frequently feel that others avoid them but are never quite sure why.

Assertive people generally stand up for their own rights and needs in ways that do not infringe on the rights of others. Assertive people are open, honest, and direct in their dealings with others, and, as much as possible, tend to feel confident in a wide variety of situations. No matter what happens, assertive people usually tend to feel good about themselves and others.

BEHAVIORAL COMPONENTS

Becoming assertive often is more than understanding the definitions and the related feelings; it frequently involves actual change in behaviors which are not consistent with assertiveness. The Behavioral Components chart (Reference A) outlines each of three modes of behavior—assertive, aggressive, and passive. Note that there are both verbal and nonverbal behaviors described. It is important to remember than an assertive verbal message must be accompanied by assertive nonverbal messages. Eye contact, posture, the use of hands, facial expressions, and energy level all communicate as much to another person as the actual words one may use. In the job interview, for example, others will be looking at *how* you conduct yourself as closely as they will listen to *what* you say.

A good way to check out how consistent your verbal and nonverbal messages are is to find a friend who will work with you as you try out some typical interview questions (see Endicott, Reference B). Have the friend give feedback on both your nonverbal and verbal messages. The role play checklist (Reference C) is helpful in this type of activity and provides some specific points of which you may wish to become aware in your interactions with others. You might also try using some sample sentences and work on developing consistent verbal and non-verbal behaviors. For example, try saying, "I am angry with you," in a way that will clearly communicate, both verbally and nonverbally, that you are angry. How about

"No, I don't want to do that!" Saying "no" to someone is often difficult, particularly if you feel the other person might not like you if you say no.

PROBLEM AREAS

All of us have different situations in which we have difficulty being assertive. For some of us, it is in social interactions with strangers; for others, in interactions with good friends. Still others have difficulty saying "no" even to unreasonable requests. It is important that one become aware of the areas which are most likely to present difficulty. Remember, few of us are totally unassertive or totally assertive—we all need to work on developing new and more effective responses to those situations, people, or circumstances which present an "assertive challenge."

The Rathus Assertiveness Schedule (See Reference D) will assist you in assessing your own level of assertiveness and will also help you identify some areas in which you might like to work. The best way to develop more assertive behaviors is, of course, to involve yourself in an ongoing group or workshop. If, however, you are not able to take the time, you can do some assessment and work independently. A bibliography of recommended readings appears at the end of this chapter.

SOME GENERAL GUIDELINES

As you begin to look at your own levels of assertiveness and the areas you may wish to change in some way, it is important to remember that becoming appropriately assertive does not mean that you will automatically get your own way. Many people are disappointed when, after acting in an assertive manner, they discover they did not get exactly what they wanted. Being assertive merely increases the possibility of getting what you want—it does not carry any guarantees! Another important point is the recognition that becoming assertive involves making choices. Just because a person has the option to be assertive does not mean he will *choose* to act assertively. In each situation and set of circumstances one must make a choice. Sometimes, it is legitimate not to be assertive.

Being assertive means learning to talk in terms of "I" statements rather than "you" statements. This means examining your own pattern of speech and determining whether or not you routinely attach "ownership" to your wants and needs. Do you usually begin with "I" or "You?" Remember, an "I" statement implies ownership of the feelings or thought you wish to convey; a "you" statement is often accusatory or implies an attack on the other person. "You" statements frequently produce a defensive response. Use "I" statements as much as possible in interactions with others.

Finally, becoming assertive involves changing long-standing patterns of behavior. If you change, others around you may be forced to change, too. This may present some problems initially, so enter into assertion training and behavior change with a bit of caution—be prepared to help those around you understand what it is you are trying to do. In many cases, your friends can become allies who will aid you in the process of becoming assertive and support you as you try new ways of interacting.

THE JOB SEARCH

About now you may be wondering about how all of this can assist you with interviewing for a job. First of all, *assertion training provides an active approach to a situation—any situation.* As you approach the job interview, prepare for it. Gather information. Anticipate some of the questions you may be asked. Prepare some of your own questions. Define some goals for yourself that you hope to meet in your first full-time job. Be able to specify these goals to a prospective employer.

Assess your own abilities with regard to the job for which you're interviewing. Be aware of your skills, limitations, frustration level and other personal characteristics. Again, be able to share this information openly and directly with a prospective employer. Sometimes knowing your own limits is as important as selling your skills.

Enter the interview situation well-rested and, as much as possible, in charge of any anxieties and fears you may have. Relax yourself as much as possible before the interview. Do what you can to minimize the stress of interviewing. Recognize that you have control only over how you present yourself and not over how the interviewer may choose to behave or respond to you. Many people create all kinds of tension by trying to anticipate every possible contingency that might appear in the interview; this is almost impossible, so prepare as well as you can and don't worry about what you might not know. Own up to lack of information directly if you don't know something.

Focus on interacting with the interviewer as you interact with people in general. In other words, be yourself. Be as open, honest, and direct in your statements as you can. Convey as much of your personal "style" as you can within the confines of the interview setting. Although the interview is not a personality contest, the openness with which you communicate will be noted.

Keep in touch with the fact that you are also interviewing the prospective employer. Ask questions if you have any and be prepared to gather information from the interviewer regarding the job, the company, and specific expectations of performance on the job. Here is where some good preparation can help you identify some things about which you may want to ask questions.

SUMMARY

Learning to behave in certain ways can benefit you in a number of areas, both personally and professionally. Like all behavior change, however, learning to be assertive involves time, energy, and commitment on your part. For most people, simply becoming aware of what we say and how we say it will improve the quality of our interactions with others; there are, however, "problem" areas and people which are difficult for each of us.

Through role-playing, enlisting the support and assistance of friends or spouses, and detailed preparation, one can learn to respond assertively in most situations and to most people. Use available resources, including assertion training, to help you prepare.

Prepared by Glenda Belote, Coordinator of Women's Services, The Ohio State University

	NON-ASSERTIVE	ASSERTIVE	AGGRESSIVE
I. VERBAL	Apologetic words. Veiled meanings. Hedging, failure to come to the point. Rambling, disconnected. At loss for words. Failure to say what you really mean. "I mean," "You know."	Statement of wants. Honest statement of feelings. Objective words. Direct statements which say what you mean. "I" messages.	"Loaded" words. Accusations. Descriptive, subjective terms. Imperious, superior words. "You"—messages, that blame or label.
II. NON-VERBAL A. General	Actions instead of words. Hoping someone will guess what you want. Looking as if you don't mean what you say.	Attentive listening behavior. General assured manner, communicating caring and strength.	Exaggerated show of strength. Flippant, sarcastic style. Air of superiority.
B. Specific 1. Voice	Weak, hesitant, soft, sometimes wavering.	Firm, warm, well-modulated, relaxed.	Tense, shrill, loud, shaky, cold, "deadly quiet"; demanding, superior, authoritarian.
2. Eyes	Averted, downcast, teary, pleading.	Open, frank, direct.	Expressionless, narrowed, cold, staring, not really "seeing" you.
3. Stance and Posture	Lean for support, stooped, excessive head nodding.	Well-balanced, straight-on, erect, relaxed.	Hands on hips, feet apart. Stiff and rigid, rude, imperious.
4. Hands	Fluttery, fidgety, clammy.	Relaxed motions.	Clenched, abrupt gestures, finger-pointing, fist pounding.

*Credit given to *The New Assertive Woman*, by Bloom, Coburn, and Pearlman, 1975.

QUESTIONS FREQUENTLY ASKED
DURING THE EMPLOYMENT INTERVIEW

As reported by 92 companies surveyed by Frank S. Endicott,
Director of Placement, Northwestern University.

1. What are your future vocational plans?
2. In what school activities have you participated? Why? Which did you enjoy the most?
3. How do you spend your spare time? What are your hobbies?
4. In what type of position are you most interested?
5. Why do you think you might like to work for our company?
6. What jobs have you held? How were they obtained and why did you leave?
7. What courses did you like best? Least? Why?
8. Why did you choose your particular field of work?
9. What percentage of your college expenses did you earn? How?
10. How did you spend your vacations while in school?
11. What do you know about our company?
12. Do you feel that you have received a good general training?
13. What qualifications do you have that make you feel that you will be successful in your field?
14. What extracurricular offices have you held?
15. What are your ideas on salary?
16. How do you feel about your family?
17. How interested are you in sports?
18. If you were starting college all over again, what courses would you take?
19. Do you prefer any specific geographic location? Why?
20. Do you date anyone regularly? Is it serious?
21. How much money do you hope to earn at age 30? 35?
22. Why did you decide to go to this particular school?
23. Do you think that your extracurricular activities were worth the time you devoted to them? Why?
24. What do you think determines a person's progress in a good company?
25. What personal characteristics are necessary for success in your chosen field?
26. Why do you think you would like this particular type of job?
27. What are your parents' occupations?
28. Tell me about your home life during the time you were growing up.
29. Do you prefer working with others or by yourself?
30. What kind of boss do you prefer?
31. Are you primarily interested in making money or do you feel that service to humanity is your prime concern?
32. Can you take instructions without feeling upset?
33. Tell me a story!
34. Do you live with your parents? Which of your parents has had the most profound influence on you?

35. How did previous employers treat you?
36. What have you learned from some of the jobs you have held?
37. Can you get recommendations from previous employers?
38. What interests you about our product or service?
39. What was your record in military service?
40. Have you ever changed your major field of interest while in college? Why?
41. When did you choose your college major?
42. Do you feel you have done the best scholastic work of which you are capable?
43. How did you happen to go to college?
44. What do you know about opportunities in the field in which you are trained?
45. Have you ever had any difficulty getting along with fellow students and faculty?
46. Which of your college years was the most difficult?
47. What is the source of your spending money?
48. Do you own any life insurance?
49. Have you saved any money?
50. Do you have any debts?
51. How old were you when you became self-supporting?
52. Did you enjoy your four years at the university?
53. Do you like routine work?
54. Do you like regular hours?
55. What size city do you prefer?
56. What is your major weakness?
57. Define cooperation!
58. Do you demand attention?
59. Do you have an analytical mind?
60. Are you eager to please?
61. What do you do to keep in good physical condition?
62. Have you had any serious illness or injury?
63. Are you willing to go where the company sends you?
64. What job in our company would you choose if you were entirely free to do so?
65. What types of books have you read?
66. Have you plans for graduate work?
67. What types of people seem to rub you the wrong way?
68. Do you enjoy sports as a participant? As an observer?
69. Have you ever tutored an underclassman?
70. What jobs have you enjoyed the most? The least? Why?
71. What are your own special abilities?
72. What job in our company do you want to work toward?
73. Would you prefer a large or small company? Why?
74. Do you like to travel?
75. How about overtime work?

76. What kind of work interests you?
77. What are the disadvantages of your chosen field?
78. Are you interested in research?
79. If married, how often do you entertain at home?
80. What have you done which shows initiative and willingness to work?

Note: If you take the time necessary to write out brief answers to each of the questions in Endicott's list, it can help you clarify your own thinking and establish ready answers.

RATING SHEET FOR OBSERVERS OF ASSERTIVENESS ROLE-PLAYS

1. Did the person establish good eye contact?

1 _____ 5

| Looked away, | Looked directly |
| down at the floor | at other person |

2. What was the general body posture?

1 _____ 5

| Leaning away, | Leaning forward, |
| slumped | erect |

3. Were hand gestures used?

1 _____ 5

| Nervous, tense | Emphatic, strong |
| movements | gestures |

4. What were the facial expressions?

1 _____ 5

| Smiling, | Calm, serious |
| laughing | expression |

5. How did the person's voice sound?

1 _____ 5

| Whispered, | Strong, clear |
| monotone | tone |

6. When did the person respond with his/her statements?

1 _____ 5

| Hesitated, long | Immediate, concise |
| pauses, use of "uh" | response |

7. What was the content of the person's statements?

1 _____ 5

| Apologies, use | Appropriate expression |
| of questions | of feelings and decision |

8. Did you notice any "hooks" used during the role play?
   —Use of guilt, loss of friendship — "Don't you like me anymore?
     "You're not being a very good friend."
   — Appeal to responsibility — "But it's your job."
   — Attempting to change the issue
   — Others

RATHUS ASSERTIVENESS SCHEDULE

Directions: Indicate how characteristic or descriptive each of the following statements is of you by using the code given below.

+3 = *very characteristic of me, extremely descriptive*
+2 = *rather characteristic of me, quite descriptive*
+1 = *somewhat characteristic of me, slightly descriptive*
-1 = *somewhat uncharacteristic of me, slightly nondescriptive*
-2 = *rather uncharacteristic of me, quite nondescriptive*
-3 = *very uncharacteristic of me, extremely nondescriptive*

+2 1. Most people seem to be more aggressive and assertive than I am.*

-2 2. I have hesitated to make or accept dates because of "shyness".*

-2 3. When the food served at a restaurant is not done to my satisfaction, I complain about it to the waiter or waitress.

+1 4. I am careful to avoid hurting other people's feelings, even when I feel that I have been injured.*

-3 5. If a salesman has gone to considerable trouble to show me merchandise which is not quite suitable, I have a difficult time in saying "NO".*

-2 6. When I am asked to do something, I insist upon knowing why.

-1 7. There are times when I look for a good, vigorous argument.

+2 8. I strive to get ahead as well as most people in my position.

+2 9. To be honest, people often take advantage of me.*

+2 10. I often don't know what to say to attractive persons of the opposite sex.*

+1 12. I will hesitate to make phone calls to business establishments and institutions.*

+2 13. I would rather apply for a job or for admission to a college by writing letters than by going through with personal interviews.*

+2 14. I find it embarrassing to return merchandise.*

+1 15. If a close and respected relative were annoying me, I would smother my feelings rather than express my annoyance.*

+3 16. I have avoided asking questions for fear of sounding stupid.*

-3 17. During an argument I am sometimes afraid that I will get so upset that I will shake all over.*

-3 18. If a famed and respected lecturer makes a statement which I think is incorrect, I will have the audience hear my point of view as well.

+2 19. I avoid arguing over prices with clerks and salesmen.*

+2 20. When I have done something important or worthwhile, I manage to let others know about it.

+3 21. I am open and frank about my feelings.

+2 22. If someone has been spreading false and bad stories about me, I see him (her) as soon as possible to "have a talk" about it.

+1 23. I often have a hard time saying "NO".*

-2 24. I tend to bottle up my emotions rather than make a scene.*

-2 25. I complain about poor service in a restaurant and elsewhere.

+1 26. When I am given a compliment, I sometimes just don't know what to say.*

+1 27. If a couple near me in a theatre or at a lecture were conversing rather loudly, I would ask them to be quiet or to take their conversation elsewhere.

-1 28. Anyone attempting to push ahead of me in a line is in for a good battle.

+1 29. I am quick to express an opinion.

+1 30. There are times when I just can't say anything.*

Scoring of the Rathus Assertiveness Schedule

1. Indicate how characteristic or descriptive each of the statements is of you by using the code given.
2. Reverse the signs of the starred (*) items. For instance, if you gave yourself a +2 on number 1 ("Most people seem to be more aggressive and assertive than I am"), you would add that as a –2.
3. Total up the +'s and the –'s. Determine the difference between the totals using the sign of the larger number. Relate your score to the following table to determine your degree of assertiveness.

Score

–15 to +15 .... Normal Range

Less than –30 .... More passive than the average person

More than +30 .... More assertive than the average person

–2	+2
–2	+3
–1	+2
–2	+2
–1	+2
–1	+2
–2	+3
–1	+3
–3	+2
–2	+3
–1	+2
–2	+2
–1	+1
–1	+1
–1	
–23	+30

+7

Credit given to *The New Assertive Woman*, by Bloom, Coburn, and Pearlman, 1975.

CHAPTER 2   Matters of Pen & Paper
The Resume & Letter of Application

Having the proper tools in hand will make your job-finding much easier. The tools that will help you get interviews are the resume and the letter of application. These documents introduce you to an employer and, if carefully prepared, will spark an interest in hiring you.

THE RESUME

The resume is a summary of your personal qualifications for a particular job. It provides valuable information about you to your employer. The resume serves as a basis for your job interview by telling the interviewer who you are, the job you want, and your special assets. The appearance of your resume makes a non-verbal statement about you also. In short, your resume advertises you.

There is no prescribed formula for the resume. You have the opportunity to present yourself uniquely. However, employers do have expectations and a set of principles in mind as they look over your resume.

The resume must be readable and provide the information an employer is looking for. Usually this includes:

— Personal identification
— Job objective
— Education
— Work experience
— Extracurricular activities
— Hobbies and interests
— References

The following Resume Worksheet will give you specific information about each of the components in your resume. It is a guide to help you collect the proper information for your resume. After you have collected the proper information, you must present it attractively and efficiently to your prospective employer.

Because employers have so many resumes to read, most want a one-page resume. The information should be presented concisely to conserve reading time. Short statements replace complete sentences or a prose style. It is assumed that you are talking about yourself so it is not necessary to use the pronoun, "I". Spelling or grammatical errors reflect upon your education and therefore, your qualifications. Careful proofreading by you and another person can protect you from giving the impression that you are ignorant, or at best, careless. Organize your resume so that the highlights are easily read by the employer who is skimming. Headings should distinguish and separate specific material in the resume.

First impressions are crucial. Remember yours is probably not the only resume to cross the employer's desk. An investment in footwork to find just the right paper, typing, and copying service can pay off in terms of a distinctive presentation of your qualifications.

Good quality paper is usually 2-pound weight and has a 25% rag content. Subtle texture and color can be very effective in setting your resume apart from others. Stationery stores, copy services, and office supply stores are good places to find attractive paper and usually matching envelopes in which to send your resume and cover letter. You will need several copies of each resume you prepare.

A good original of your resume will insure a good reproduction. Strive for the greatest contrast between paper and type. A new ribbon, or better yet, a carbon or film ribbon on very white paper gives the high contrast necessary for sharp reproduction. The original can then be reproduced on the paper of your choice. Choose a readable type face also. Italic or script is hard to read. You can experiment with press-on letters to give added emphasis to headings or titles in your resume.

Though the resume helps the employer find out about you, preparing the resume helps you, too. You gain poise before the interview because you have thoroughly analyzed your life and organized your experiences with the job you want in mind. You have confidence because the facts you need to document your experience and qualifications are fresh in your mind. As you gain experience and update your resume, the process will help you assess the progress you have or have not made toward your goals.

LETTER OF APPLICATION

When you send a resume to a prospective employer, you should always preface it with a letter. This letter is called a letter of application, a cover letter, or a letter of transmittal. In this letter, you make your initial introduction to the employer. You let him know why you are interested in his employment opportunity, direct him to your resume which explains your qualifications, and ask for an interview to discuss your qualifications further.

Though your resume is aimed toward a specific kind of job, it is not aimed toward a specific employer. The letter of application serves to tie your resume in with a specific employer by highlighting particular experiences or qualities that directly link you to the job available.

The letter of application is the place to mention things about yourself that do not fit well in the resume. For instance, where in the resume would you communicate that you understand and accept that you will have to start at the bottom but that you want to move up? Or, where do you mention that you are willing to work hard? If you have an apparent personal limitation, such as a physical handicap, and are concerned with an unfavorable first impression, you may wish to mention this briefly in your letter. Although an employer may not discriminate against you because of your limitation, you may want to reassure him or her that you are capable before the job interview when first impressions are at stake. Of course, you should explain that your problem is under control, how you have worked around your problem in the past, and how you will in your future job, too. Be specific and realistic.

A guide has been included in this book that explains the different components of the cover letter. It is only a guide to help with form and general information. Do not be afraid to individualize!

WHAT TO INCLUDE IN THE LETTER

Addresses. Your goal is to get the employer to contact you for an interview. Make it easy for him by including your full address at the top of the letter. The exact placement depends upon the format you have chosen to use. Letterhead stationery can be printed to create a distinguishing effect. The inside address is the address of the person to whom you are writing. It is placed right above the salutation and is the same address that is used on the mailing envelope.

Know a name to write if at all possible. You know what receiving a letter marked "Occupant" does for you. Addressing a letter to "Director of Personnel," "Department of Employment," or "Director" evokes the same reaction. Some sleuthing can help you come up with the name you need! A few places to look are:

— Employees presently with the firm
— Placement offices
— Corporation's annual report
— Company and surrounding community
— Newspaper articles
— Library at your college or university
— Business and Technology division of your public library's collection of directories which may provide corporate addresses, officers

Business Services — General Directories:

— *Directory of Corporate Affiliations*
— *Directory of Inter-corporate Ownership*
— *Directory of Obsolete Securities*
— *Dun & Bradstreet Middle Market Directory*
— *Dun & Bradstreet Million Dollar Directory*
— *Dun & Bradstreet Reference Book of Corporate Managements*
— *Encyclopedia of Associations*
— *MacCrae's Blue Book*
— *Marketing Economics Key Plants*
— *Penny Stock Handbook*
— *Robert D. Fisher Manual of Valuable and Worthless Securities*
— *Standard & Poor's Register of Corporations, Directors and Executives*
— *Standard Directory of Advertisers*
— *30,000 Leading U.S. Corporations*
— *Thomas Register of American Manufacturers*

The Salutation. The salutation follows the inside address and is always punctuated with a colon. (Examples: Dear Ms. Lighter:, Dear Dr. Sand:) Again, knowing a name will help you get around the awkward problem of Dear Sir or Madam. (In general business correspondence, if you do not know a name, it is acceptable to write Dear Sir: or Dear Madam:).

The Body. What you put in the body of the letter is up to you. You should supply the information necessary to fulfill the purposes of the letter. Try to avoid making your letter read like a form letter — direct it specifically to the organization. Some general suggestions are:

— To paraphrase John F. Kennedy, emphasize what you can do for the company, not what they can do for you.

— Be clear about what job you want.

— Tie your resume to the specific organization to which you are applying.

— Emphasize specifics in your personal background that qualify you for the job.

— Request the next step and suggest how it can be done. Example: "I will be in your area July 5-10 and would like to schedule an interview at that time."

Closing. "Sincerely," "Yours truly" are acceptable closing phrases. Always sign your name. Use ink. Type your name below your signature.

As in the resume, aesthetic considerations can distinguish your letter from others. Since you send the two documents together, the paper for your cover letter should match the paper you used for your resume. When you have your resume copied, ask for a supply of blank paper for your letters. Most of the time, matching envelopes are also available.

You may wish to match type styles in your resume and letter of application. Remember, however, that the resume can be reproduced but the cover letter is always an original.

Do not detract from your qualifications with poor spelling, grammar or punctuation. Proofread. If you are not sure about these details, consult an English handbook or ask an expert.

The form of a letter of application is the same as for any business letter. A guide has been included in this book to help you with margins and spacing. It is not a prescription for cover letters but can help you produce an attractive finished product.

RESUME WORKSHEET

The following worksheet was designed to help you collect the appropriate information for your resume. It will help you inventory and select experiences you have had that will most enhance your job prospects.

IDENTIFICATION

Name _____

Permanent address_____
　　　　　　　　　　　Street　　　　City　　　　State　　Zip Code

Telephone _____
　　　　　　　Area Code

School Address_____
　　　　　　　　　　Street　　　　City　　　　State　　Zip Code

Telephone _____
　　　　　　　Area Code

■ *Principle:* *Make sure it is easy for a prospective employer to contact you.*

PROFESSIONAL OBJECTIVES
After self-assessment, write several job objectives that fit you. Make them specific.

1. _____

_____

2. _____

_____

3. _____

_____

4. _____

_____

Now, clip several job descriptions that interest you. Line them up with your professional objectives. Which ones match? Use the objective from your list that most closely matches the job you are interested in getting. Obviously, this may change from job to job. That leads to the next principle.

■ *Principle:* *Have several different resumes on hand and use the one that best matches the job for which you are applying.*

EDUCATION
Degree earned _____

Major

Institution _____

        Name   *City*   *State*

Special projects (such as honors, independent study, research) or educational experiences that will enhance your job performance (such as field or tional experiences that will enhance your job performance (such as field work or student teaching). Be specific. What did you learn and how will it help you on the job?

_____

_____

_____

_____

_____

_____

_____

_____

_____

_____

_____

School honors_____

_____

_____

_____

Is your information correct? Be sure you are accurate in designation of names and titles.

- ■ **Principle:** *Education is listed in either reverse chronological order or chronological order. Be consistent.*

- ■ **Principle:** *Before a couple of years of work experience, education will precede work experience on your resume. After a couple of years of work experience, the work experience should be listed first.*

EXTRACURRICULAR
Describe the extracurricular activities you participated in during school. It will give the prospective employer information about your ability to get along with people, leadership abilities, interests, enthusiasm and energy levels.

(Students returning after a long absence from school should emphasize extracurricular activities because many times organizational skills gained match skills needed on the job.)

Name of Organization _____

Offices held _____

Experiences gained_____

_____

_____

_____

_____

_____

How did you benefit the organization?_____

_____

_____

_____

_____

Name of organization _____

Offices held _____

Experiences gained_____

_____

_____

_____

How did you benefit the organization? _____

_____

_____

_____

_____

WORK EXPERIENCE
Emphasize aspects of job experience that affect your job objective for this

resume — for instance, experience with people, gaining understanding of different levels of organizations, or meeting deadlines. Get the idea? Almost every job experience you have had has helped you gain something that will make you a more valuable employee in future jobs.   It is a good idea to do this for each job you have held.

Employer _____

Location_____

Dates of employment _____ to _____

mo./yr.   mo./yr.

Title _____

Brief description of responsibilities _____

_____

_____

_____

Employer _____

Location _____

Dates of employment _____ to _____

mo./yr.   mo./yr.

Title _____

Brief description of responsibilities _____

_____

_____

_____

- ■ **Principle:** *On your resume, list work experience in reverse chrono-logical order, i.e., most recent job experience first. An alternate approach is to list experience in order according to its relationship to the job you want. This is called the "functional approach."*

- ■ **Principle:** *Emphasize aspects of your job experiences that are related to the job you want.*

A SPECIAL NOTE

Adult returning students with a considerable lapse in paid employment should emphasize any organizational skills they have developed in the interim. The same skills that make one a valuable volunteer worker make one a valuable paid employee. Describe volunteer work in the same way as you would paid employment experience. Be specific about how you benefitted the organization.

INTERESTS, HOBBIES, PERSONAL INFORMATION

This information gives an interviewer a conversational starting point. It also rounds you out as a total person and can give the employer clues about your personality.

_____

_____

_____

_____

_____

_____

REFERENCES

Though you _do not_ include this information in your resume, you will want to keep a record of your references.

Name _____
                                    Relationship to you

Address _____
         Street   _City_   _State_   _Zip Code_

Telephone _____
           Area Code

Name _____
                                    Relationship to you

Address _____
         Street   _City_   _State_   _Zip Code_

Telephone _____
           Area Code

Name _____
                                    Relationship to you

Address _____
         Street   _City_   _State_   _Zip Code_

Telephone _____
           Area Code

- ***Principle:*** *Make use of the placement office services.*
- ***Principle:*** *Choose someone who knows your work abilities.*
- ***Principle:*** *Choose someone who has known you recently when possible.*
- ***Principle:*** *Never choose a relative.*
- ***Principle:*** *Contact persons before using them as references to get their permission.*
- ***Principle:*** *Do not include actual names on the resume. State something like, "available or furnished upon request."*
- ***Principle:*** *When using the placement office, saying references are available from that office will slow down the process because the placement office must then contact you to get your permission to send materials that they have. It is faster if you contact the placement office personally upon request of a prospective employer. It is a good idea to keep references on file for this purpose in the placement office. Be sure to know the exact procedure to follow at your college or university.*

Do you feel better about your chances for employment? Somehow, it helps to organize and write down important facts about yourself to get a clear idea of what you can offer a prospective employer. This process will help in the interview, for writing letters of application, and for completing job applications. Keep the inventory up-to-date and it can greatly simplify the job-finding process in the future, as well as right now.

GUIDE FOR LETTER OF APPLICATION

Street address
City, State, Zip Code
Date

Person to whom you are writing
Title of person
Company name
Street address
City, State, Zip Code

Dear (Use person's name):

First paragraph. This is the opening paragraph. Tell what position you are applying for, how you learned of the position or company, and why you are interested in working for them.

Second paragraph. Elaborate briefly on why you are the person for the job. Include information that was difficult to convey via the resume. What can you offer the company? Will you work hard? Are you willing to relocate? What features in your background make you particularly suitable for the job?

Third paragraph. Refer the person to your resume. You may highlight (briefly!!!) your summary of qualifications.

Fourth paragraph. Request the "next step." Include information that will facilitate a meeting between you and the prospective employer. End with some sort of statement or question that will encourage a reply.

Closing phrase,

Always sign your name

Your name in full

Enclosure: Resume

FORMAT GUIDE
FOR THE
LETTER OF APPLICATION

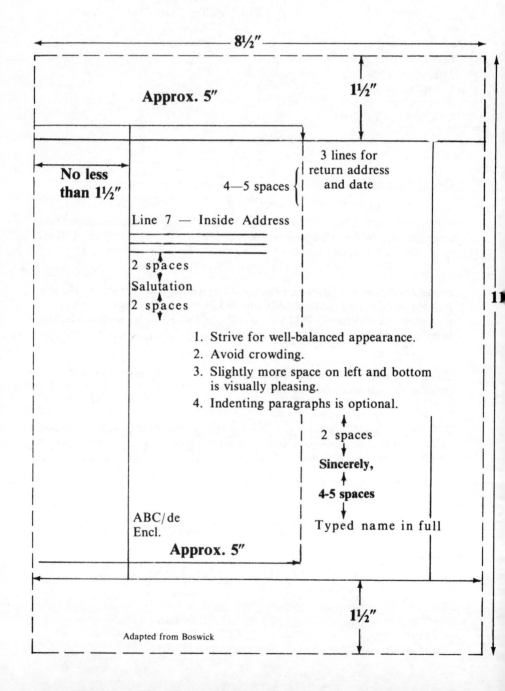

8½"

Approx. 5"

1½"

No less than 1½"

4—5 spaces

3 lines for return address and date

Line 7 — Inside Address

2 spaces
Salutation
2 spaces

1. Strive for well-balanced appearance.
2. Avoid crowding.
3. Slightly more space on left and bottom is visually pleasing.
4. Indenting paragraphs is optional.

2 spaces

Sincerely,

4-5 spaces

Typed name in full

ABC/de
Encl.

Approx. 5"

11"

1½"

Adapted from Boswick

CHAPTER 3   EMPLOYERS LOOK FOR **GOOD** EMPLOYEES

Employers are looking for a combination of ability and personality. Unless you are an undisputed genius, you won't make it with poor attitude (unwillingness to follow company policy), Casper Milquetoast personality or one of the steamroller variety. An employer must have reason to believe he can work with you. On the other hand, you may charm the employer with your suave, debonair or cutsie-pie ways, but air-heads don't stay long. Most of the traits employers look for can be characterized as those of ability or personality.

Employers look for evidence of achievement in your past records. If you have achieved once, you can probably do it again. Many employers are impressed by a fine scholastic record because they feel superior achievement is necessary for leadership and technical competence. However, low grades do not necessarily mean the end. Be able to explain your grades. For instance, those who had to support themselves through college had less time to devote to academics. Other responsibilities cut into study time also. Participation in extracurricular activities will influence grades. Do not make excuses, but be able to explain your accomplishments.

Thorough self-analysis is in order before the interview. Know what you have done and how to prove it. Determine to develop your ability with accomplishments if self-analysis discloses weaknesses in this area. It may help to be able to explain your plan for developing your abilities.

Certain kinds of abilities are important to employers. Oral and written communication skills are vital in any organization. The employer will judge your oral skill during the interview. He may look at your resume, letter of application and job application as evidence of your written communication ability. Play up any course work that dealt with communication. There are many opportunities for improvement in this area through workshops, seminars, adult education and other avenues of continued learning. Good reading will also help develop your communication skills.

What are your motives for work? Employers know that most of us work to eat, but look for something beyond this. Is your work a source of personal satisfaction? Do you have a desire to achieve? Employers want to know something of your ambitions. What are your goals and what are you doing to achieve them? How does this job fit in? Be careful about emphasizing what this job will do for you. The employer knows that. You are the one who must sell the interviewer on what you can do for the company.

Leadership counts with employers. This can be considered a personality trait but it is also a result of an ability to plan and organize. The employer will look at your extracurricular activities for evidence of leadership potential. Do not forget to mention activities that were not school-related. Leadership is required in church and community organizations also.

Employers are looking for persons with high energy levels. He may have to make a decision about your enthusiasm and interest level on the basis of the job interview. That is why it is important to be alert, rested, and "peppy." The employer wants to know whether or not you are willing to work hard and extra if it means getting a task done properly. Asking many questions during the interview about vacation and leave time may make the employer a bit anxious about your willingness to work. What kind of work standards do you have? Information about your work standards will come through in your recommendations. You can supplement this with a good portfolio of samples of your work.

What evidence do you have to demonstrate your ability to get along and work with others? Employers need to know this. Personality characteristics are usually evaluated on the basis of the interview. No matter what happens in the interview, do not explode in an angry outburst or become sullen. You never know who the employer knows or what he may turn up later. *Remember* it is sometimes the intent of the interviewer to see if you can handle pressure and still be civil. Prove that you can.

What, then, do employers look for? *A good employee.* Because the job interview and application procedures are a skimpy basis for making a decision about your "employee-manship," you are going to have to work hard to present yourself in this light. Know your abilities, accomplishments and what you can do. Know where you are headed. Know that you can get along with others and how to support this. In other words, *know yourself* so your employer can.

INTERVIEWS

An employer needs an employee and you need a job. The purpose of the selection or job interview is to fulfill both of your needs. The interview is a business deal in a way, also. The employer wants to get to know you better and to find out whether or not he can "live with you." You likewise, must decide if this is the position you want and whether or not you can contribute to the organization.

For some jobs, selection interviewing involves several interviews. For these jobs, you are first screened and then, upon passing this point, are interviewed by higher levels of management before a final decision is reached. Employers are interested in persons who can tolerate stress. Time pressure, opposition of ideas, group pressures and difficulty of tasks are pressures inherent in some jobs. During the preliminary screening, you may encounter a **stress interview.** The interviewer may ask rapid-fire questions, make derogatory remarks, or remain sullenly silent for long periods of time. Try to control your mental and physical squirming. Calmly and matter-of-factly answer his questions. Becoming angry or crying is a good indication that you cannot handle stress.

Remember that the employment interview, like any other conversation, is an exchange. Have questions ready that you want answered. Be prepared so that you can participate.

A successful job interview is usually a result of careful planning. As in the resume and letter of application, you must know with whom you are communicating.

Preliminary Sleuthing: Analysis of Prospective Employers

You would be surprised at the number of job applicants who participate in hiring interviews knowing very little about their prospective employer. The job interview is relatively short, approximately 30 minutes. Do not waste this time getting information you should have beforehand. You will compare favorably with competitors if you do some preliminary analysis of whom you wish to work for. Library sources, newspapers, professional publications, placement officers, conversations with employees, persons in the community and others will give you the information you need to complete this form which will arm you for your competent image.

This analysis will also clue you in on what kind of person the organization employs, dress standards and general personality of the firm. You can use all of these clues in your job interview.

Who is the Employer?

Name of employer and organization
Address of main office
Geographical distribution of branches and subsidiaries (It will not hurt to
    have a good argument in mind for the location you prefer.)
Nature of the organization
Reason organization exists
Major efforts of organization

Size of organization
Overall climate of organization (i.e., progressive, conservative, futuristic, etc.)
Financial status
  Annual income
  Sources of income
  Market served or to whom are services directed?
  Average annual budget
  Net worth
How does the employer/organization stand in relation to others?
Competitors
  Location
  Major number
Who are key personnel?
  Chief authority
  Organizational framework
  Interests of key personnel (i.e., pet projects, concerns, missions)
  Department heads, supervisors for whom you might work
  Personnel officer
Occupations within the organization?
  Specific jobs that interest you
  Salary range
  Beginner's jobs
      Salary range
  Career ladder
  Promotion policies
  Hiring practices
Benefits of organization
  Training programs
  Educational update requirements
  Fringe benefits
  Extracurricular functions or activities you are expected to fulfill
Special projects of organization
  Sponsorships (i.e., youth organizations, charities, programs, etc.)
What about the interview?
  Location
  Directions for getting there
  Parking
  Time of interview
  Interviewer's name
  Interviewer's characteristics, values, biases, interests
  Relationship of interviewer to you after hiring

First Impressions
  The first one to five minutes of your interview are crucial. You will trigger the employer's personal biases — his "hidden agenda." Think of your reactions upon first meeting someone. The employer is no different. The first impression determines whether or not this hidden agenda is working in your favor or whether you will have to work harder to overcome initial biases. Employers

Major source: Nutter, Caroly, *The Resume Workbook*, 4th Ed., Cranston, Rhode Island: Carrol Press, 1970.

need people who can make good first impressions. Organizations need people who can make good first impressions, too.

Being late will probably make a strong first impression — one you may never overcome. Know the exact location, time and place for the interview. Remember to make allowances for Murphy's Law when trying to get somewhere on time. Know where you are going to park. You do not want to be madly circling the building at the last minute — it will probably put your mind in circles.

> **MURPHY'S LAW**
> *Everything that can possibly go wrong,*
> *will, and at the worst possible time.*

Seasoned interviewers will discount a certain amount of nervousness, so don't get nervous about your nervousness. Before walking into the interviewer's office, take several deep breaths. Exhale slowly, and gear up mentally. Of course, you do not want to make this little exercise a public display. Before you end up in a basket somewhere, remember the employer desperately wants a good person to fill the job he has. You are helping him out.

You will be marketing yourself, so to speak, in the employment interview. If you have done your preliminary research and found everything you could about the company, you will have a good idea of the image you need to project. Clothes are a means of projecting this image. You may feel that what's you is you and the company will have to accept you. Weigh the value of your individuality against the risk of distraction in the interview. Clothing makes a statement about your attitude and your willingness to follow company policy. Choose clothing for the interview using the same principles you would to choose clothing for on the job. Generally, neat and conservative is the safe way to go. For the interview, you especially want to wear something that makes you feel confident — so well put together that you can forget about what you are wearing. Whatever you wear, wear it neatly. If the prospective employer thinks you care enough about yourself to put forth a neat appearance on the interview, he may infer that you would exercise the same care on the job. He has nothing else to go on.

You probably have heard a lot about body language in recent years. Be aware of your own nonverbal expression during the videotape practice interview in the course, and work on areas in which you are deficient. Nonverbal communication will either support or contradict what you are saying verbally. Eye contact is good, but don't overdo it. You have heard that most people want others to look them in the eye. It would be more accurate to say that most people want others to look them straight in the eye — most of the time. Do not make the interviewer uncomfortable by an unbroken stare. He may feel you are arrogant or hostile. Many times, too much eye contact is not the problem as often as is too little eye contact. If you have problems looking someone straight in the eye, try looking them straight in the nose, or more specifically, straight in the bridge of the nose. Employers will value honest enthusiasm for a job. Energy levels are shown through the rate, tone and quality of your speaking voice. Practice. An audio or videotaped practice interview will help you assess your speaking voice. Energy also shows in the way you walk. Practice walking confidently and straight. Think about some accomplishment of which you are proud — how does this affect your walk? You may want to mentally gear up before walking into the interviewer's office. Honesty is hard to fake. The more you try to hide a strong feeling, the more your body will betray you. Instead, try stating your strong feelings calmly, tactfully and openly. Hopefully, your prospective employer will respect you for it. Controlling your mental state is the key to controlling your non-verbal signs. Concentrate on the positive aspects of the job interview. What do you like about your interviewer? About the job? What do you like about yourself? What positive contributions can you make to this organization? Think of these things and body language won't be a problem.

EMPLOYMENT INTERVIEWS

Phase I

The *introductory phase* is the ice-breaking part of your meeting. Sometimes the employer gets a few conversational leads from your resume. Sometimes he'll say something like, "Well, tell me about yourself." Having done your homework, you'll tell him about yourself in a way that relates to the job. The introductory phase of the interview is non-threatening. You are both loosening up to get down to business. Be friendly but serious and smile when you can.

Phase II

The second phase of the interview, or the body, is an *exchange of information*. First, the interviewer will discuss your background and qualifications in order to measure your appropriateness for the position. Most of the time, this is a question and answer time. See the sample questions following the chapter on assertiveness. Have your answers prepared and thought through. You should have an idea in advance about what qualifications are necessary for the position. Surprise the interviewer with some intelligent questions of your own to amplify what you already know about the company. State your positive qualifications concretely — I did this and I did that. Let the employer infer what a wonderful employee you would be.

Be aware of your limitations and be prepared to discuss them frankly along with a plan for coping with them. A good example is given in *Making the Most of Your Job Interview:*

Interviewer: "Do you always pitch right into an assignment and get it done ahead of time?"

Interviewee: "I don't always get assignments done before they are due. I sometimes tend to put things off until they have to be done. However, I have never turned in a major assignment or term paper that was late."

If you have a physical handicap, you are going to have to assure the interviewer of your capabilities. Have a coping plan clearly organized in your mind.

While yes/no answers may imply that you are frightened into being tonguetied, or that you do not know any more than yes or no, or that you do not like to talk to the interviewer, long-windedness will not help your case either. Answer questions fully and concisely. You will be able to do this if you have anticipated and planned answers. If not, the tendency is to talk and talk until you think of something to say. Take your time to think through difficult questions. If you do not know the answer to a question, say so. You can offer to find out. Do not reiterate what you've said.

In the tension of the interview, many people lapse into repetition. In some people's conversation, "hmmm," "okays," and "you knows" occur at regular intervals. Okay, it becomes regularly annoying, you know. Watch overuse of the interviewer's name. John Carnegie probably had a good idea but his overzealous followers seem to have sincerity deficiencies.

What if an employer asks you an illegal question? The questions such as: "How old are you?"; "Are you married?"; "Do you have any savings?"; are not job related and it is within your rights not to answer them. If you choose not to answer, refuse tactfully. It may help to try to determine what is the employer's real concern. A question about your marital status may be a cover for "How long can we expect you to be here?" Answering the real concern may buffer your refusal to answer the impertinent question. Consider also, that the employer may be trying to antagonize you in a stress situation or may be testing your alertness. Let your own poise guide you.

During the body of the interview, the employer has gotten information about you. He will probably ask you if you have any questions about the company. Do not be afraid to ask for clarification. Remember, this is a participatory activity.

The question of salary may come up. Know what the going rate for this position is. Some writers advocate a bargaining process for determining salary. Using this process, you should have three figures in mind:

1. your baseline or absolute minimum acceptable salary,
2. your expected salary
3. your negotiating figure (expected salary plus 10%).

Ask for your negotiating figure and then bargain until you come close to your expected figure. The key to successful negotiations is to never create a win/lose situation for the employer. In other words — no ultimatums. Allow both of you a way to "keep face." If you can't seem to arrive at your expected figure, ask about salary review policies. Would you be eligible for a raise upon satisfactory performance? What about fringe benefits? Potential for advancement or other considerations may make a seemingly low salary worthwhile.

Phase III

At the close of the interview, the employer may begin explaining application procedures. He may even offer you an application. You can either take it with you or complete it in his office. It is always a good idea to take information with you that will help you complete applications — such as employment dates, names and references. If you have done your preparation well — preliminary analysis of the company, attention to appearance and adequate questioning practices — you will probably discover that an employment interview is not so bad after all.

If you feel the interview did not go well, save your discouragement for your trip home. The employer may be trying to test you or you may not qualify for this particular job. If you handle yourself well, he may remember you when a job more suited to you turns up.

WHICH WAY

COMPARING JOB OFFERS

The following scales will make it easier for you to see the pros and cons of working with various companies for which you have interviewed. These items are to channel your thinking to a more extensive evaluation of your possibilities. Scores from your "Work Values Inventory" or other similar measures will help you decide which factors are those most important to you. Space is given to enable you to keep an organized record of information you have gathered. Sometimes it helps to give a numerical (0—3 or 0—5) rating for each scale, including your value of the item. Tally your total and decide which employer is ahead.

POTENTIAL EMPLOYERS	A	B	C	D
Qualifications Required Requirements for entry				
Requirement in future and when in future				
Training programs				
scope				
sponsorship				
inservice				
continuing education				
institutes				
workshops				
conventions				
Employer Characteristics Financial status				
Growing or shrinking market?				
Growth history				
Type of service				
Market or people serviced				
Personnel policies				
Professional/employee ratio				
Professional organizations				
Job Scope and responsibilities				
Prestige				
Satisfaction and interest				
Travel				
Match with your goals				

Remuneration	A	B	C	D
Salary				
Profit sharing				
Savings, stock plan				
Taxes, retirement				
Bonuses				
Product discounts				
History of increases				
Travel expenses				
Moving expenses				
Expectations in 10 years				
Benefits				
Vacation				
Personal leave				
Sickness				
Hospitalization				
Life insurance				
Maternity leave				
Services for employees				
Child care				
Advancement				
Career ladder				
Requirements				
Merit raises				
Professionals in top management				
Advancement to other than management positions				
Train to hire from within				
Competition for advancement				
Supervision				
Personality of supervisor				
Background				
How many				
Chain of command				
Working Conditions				
Office, lab, classroom				
Equipment and supplies				
Assistance (office or secretarial help				
Flexibility in hours				
Outside time demands				
Child care				
Ratings & Recommendations				
Employees				
Relatives				
Placement Director				
Faculty				
Peers				
Others				

Geographic Location	A	B	C	D
Relocation				
How often?				
Location of branches				
Climate				
Schools				
advanced degrees				
children's				
Standard of living cost				
Community				
Access				
Cultural and religious offerings				

An actual interview is the best way to gain experic .ce in an interview situation. However, it is not always possible to gain actual experience, particularly prior to that *first* crucial interview. One way to practice interviewing is to simulate an interview situation with roommates, friends, colleagues, or teachers. Taping the interview and evaluating the playback can be especially helpful. Videotaped interviews have the advantage of revealing both **speech and body language problems which you may want to correct.**

In evaluating your practice interview consider speech quality, self confidence and poise, quality of your responses and interaction with the interviewer. The following list of questions is representative of the type that may be asked during an interview. You may also refer to the section "Questions Frequently Asked During the Employment Interview" (Reference B in "Standing Up For YOU").

1. What are your future vocational plans?
2. In what type of position are you most interested?
3. What satisfactions do you derive from a job?
4. **What jobs have you held? How were they obtained and why did you leave?**
5. Why did you choose your particular field of work?
6. Do you feel that you have received a good general training? In what way?
7. What qualifications do you have that make you feel that you will be successful in your field?
8. What is your concept of management? How do you manage?
9. What do you think determines a person's progress in a good company?
10. What personal characteristics are necessary for success in your chosen field?
11. What do you know about opportunities in the field in which you are trained?
12. What kind of work interests you?
13. What have you done which shows initiative and willingness to work?
14. Cite three of your most significant achievements during the past five years and explain why you feel they were significant.
15. What advantages does a degree in Home Economics have over a degree in business in a management-oriented job?

CHAPTER 4 PLACEMENT SERVICES

College placement offices are valuable resources for you as you begin your job search. Services offered for students and alumni include:

— assisting with career planning
— providing resources on careers and job placement
— maintaining recommendations and related records
— posting available position openings
— scheduling interviews with recruiters

The coordinator or director of the placement office is available to help you focus your search for career options suitable to you based on your education and experience. The coordinator or director may alert you to opportunities you may not have considered.

Information from professional organizations, industry and various employers is kept on file in the office. Much of this information will be useful to you as you research prospective employers for your letters of application and interview assignments. You may even gain employment leads from looking over the material.

Some college offices maintain references and related records needed when you seek or change jobs. All students, both undergraduate and graduate, are urged to register for this service before graduation and to update their records after graduation. Some offices may charge for this service. Recommendations kept on file have the added benefit of constant availability without the inconvenience and delay of asking the reference to submit recommendations for each request you have. Also, if the reference becomes unreachable for some reason, the recommendations are always on file. It is desirable to secure recommendations from each employer to add to your file. Keep your file up-to-date!!

PROCEDURE FOR REGISTRATION

Registration for the use of placement services is similar in most schools and universities. Check with the Coordinator or Director of the Placement Office at your school to determine specific registration procedures. The following example of placement services offered by the School of Home Economics at The Ohio State University may help you to more fully understand the use of the services at your school. You will want to check your school for specifics.

On The Ohio State University Columbus campus students are encouraged to register with and to use the services of the Home Economics Alumni and Placement Office (henceforth referred to as A & P). In addition, home economics education majors may want to register with and use the services of the Education Personnel Placement Office.

1. Complete Placement Data Form

A placement data form should be completed carefully, accurately and neatly, as it is duplicated and given to recruiters with whom you interview.

2. Secure Recommendations

Secure the forms for recommendations from the A & P Office. These forms will be given to you when you submit your completed Placement Data Form.

3. Distribute Recommendation Forms

Select at least three persons to serve as recommenders. You may ask current and past employers, advisors, and instructors for recommendations. Enter your name on the form prior to distributing. After distribution, check with the A & P Office to see if the recommendations have been submitted. If not, you may have to remind your references or perhaps select additional ones. It is suggested that you have at least three recommendations on file before you request them to be sent to potential employers.

A critical question for you to face prior to distributing the recommendation form is, "Should I waive my right of access" to the completed form? As you well know, "The Family Educational Rights and Privacy Act of 1974, as amended," allows you to choose whether or not you may read the recommendations. There are pros and cons. Some feel that waiving your right to review the recommendations enhances the credibility of the recommendations because the reference will not be influenced by the fact that you will read what has been written. Additionally, you are certain to ask persons whom you feel will give a favorable recommendation. You will want them to give honest recommendations. But, you must make the decision to waive or not waive individually for each reference; once the decision is made, it is permanent.

According to the Family Educational Rights and Privacy Act of 1974, as amended, no student may inspect or review: 1) confidential letters and statements of recommendation placed in education records prior to January 1, 1975; 2) confidential letters and statements of recommendation for admission, employment, or honorary recognition placed in education records after January 1, 1975, for which a student has signed a waiver of his or her right of access accorded by the Act.

In summary, if you want to review a recommendation, *do not* sign the waiver. Once you sign the waiver, you have waived your right of access to the recommendations. Any recommendations received prior to January 1, 1975 remain confidential.

4. Complete a Release Form

A signed release form must be submitted prior to each release of your recommendations. On this form you may indicate which recommendation you want released. If you feel a particular recommendation on file is detrimental, you can request that it never be released. Upon receipt of your signed release, copies of your recommendations will be sent to potential employers. The original of each is kept on file permanently. *Do not* advise potential employers to write the A & P Office directly for references and letters of recommendations. Employers first contact you for references, after which you submit a signed *Recommendation Release Form*. Requests to have recommendations sent should occur *only after* the potential employer requests such; it is not expected that the letters would be received unless the potential employer requests them. In other words, sending a resume and letter of application should not require a request for recommendation letters to be sent. A potential employer will ask you for such.

(NOTE: The procedure for the release of recommendations described here applies to the School of Home Economics, The Ohio State University.

Other placement offices may handle this procedure differently. Therefore, you should check with your school placement office for specific release
procedures.)

JOB SEARCH

The A & P Office provides yet another service to job seekers. When you
begin your job campaign, you may complete an *Active Job Search Card.*
This places you on file to be notified of position openings as they become
available. This card remains on file for six months, then is removed
unless you request that it remain active.

As a graduate you may establish or reactivate records at any time and
use the career planning and placement services. Always notify the A & P
Office of any change of name, address and/or employment.

Descriptions of position openings received by the A & P Office are filed
in *Job Books* which are open to all students and alumni. Duplicate copies
of information found in the *Job Books* are placed in the library on a weekly
basis.

RECRUITER VISITS

The A & P Office serves as a clearing house for on-campus job interviews.
The schedule for recruiter visits and sign-up times for interviews is posted
early each term. Information on organizations conducting on-campus
interviews is available. This information needs to be reviewed prior to
your interview. Since brochures cannot be checked out of the office, allow
time to review this material and take notes as needed.

Appointments are made by signing up. Sign-up time for interviews
with recruiters begins prior to the recruiter's visit. You are expected to
keep an interview appointment after you sign up. However, in the event
that you cannot keep the appointment as scheduled, cancel it as
soon as possible, so someone else may take your place.

If you do not keep an interview appointment and fail to cancel it,
interviewing privileges may be discontinued.

After reporting where instructed, you will be directed to the interviewer.
You are requested to return to the coordinator after the interview.

It is suggested that you bring a resume with you to each interview to
supplement the copy of your *Placement Data Form* that is given each
recruiter with whom you schedule an interview.

TRANSCRIPT REQUESTS

Some employers will request a copy of your transcript. This is available
for a fee through the Transcript Division, Office of Records, at your college
or university.

IN SUMMARY

— register by completing *Placement Data Form*
— secure recommendations

— distribute forms to references:
   (a) check for return of recommendations
   (b) review recommendations *if* you did not waive your "right of access"
— complete a *Release Form* each time you want recommendations sent
— complete an *"Active Job Search Card"* if you want to be notified of position openings
— notify the Alumni and Placement Office of any change of name, address and/or employment.

ADDITIONAL QUESTIONS??

You may want to schedule a conference with the placement services director at your school or university to answer additional questions you have regarding placement services.

CHAPTER 5   OVERVIEW OF CONTINUED LEARNING

Many people hold to the innoculation theory of education — one shot and it is over. As a professional, you need to avoid the diseases of stagnation and obsolescence by continual "boosters" of education. Education does not have to be in a classroom or even school affiliation. (Much of your postgraduate work will be self-education.)

Membership in a good professional organization is a good start toward keeping up with your field. Most organizations publish newsletters, journals, or other publications. Read them! Read them for the information they contain and also for notices of other educational opportunities. New books, publications, workshops, seminars and training programs are often advertised in professional journals. Some employers provide a service in which the table of contents of pertinent publications are distributed to employees. This is an invaluable service to steer you toward the reading you need.

Professional organizations also sponsor continued learning opportunities. Members receive notices of events that are geared toward maintaining the level of expertise among the membership. A list of professional organizations has been compiled for this book. Each department lists appropriate organizations. Look them over, ask faculty members for information and join up!

Your employer is also a potential source of education. Educational opportunities are a consideration in your decision about job offers. Employers will either help defray your educational expenses, provide the entire cost, or sponsor training programs, workships, or seminars in different areas.

Many organizations for women are now offering educational opportunities in money management, finance, legal aid and other topics of interest to women. Look for listings of these organizations in the telephone directory, community directories, or newspapers and call to learn of the opportunities available.

Libraries, community centers, and churches offer courses or workshops in a wide range of topics. Again, call to determine what is available to help you.

Universities offer many programs either as credit or non-credit opportunities. There is usually an Office for Continuing Education to which to direct inquiries. Graduate school is another possibility and is dealt with later in this section.

An independent reading program will be a rich source of continued learning. It requires mental discipline to stick to such a program but the benefits far exceed the cost. What are the publications in the field of your interest? These are good sources for leads for even more reading. Many professionals have prepared themselves for higher positions or positions differing from their area of expertise through a reading program. If you think about it, a personal reading program is the least expensive way to expand your knowledge and is probably the most flexible. It is also a strong discipline for your other educational pursuits. If you lack self-discipline, join a reading group with similar interests or form your own group. These groups are valuable for pooling information and simply sharing from what others have read and serving as a strong motivational force. The section on libraries will aid you in finding many reading resources.

Have you considered graduate school as a means of continuing your learning and professional development? Check the section in this chapter written about graduate school opportunities — you may find something to think about. A listing of professional organizations has been included in the book to help your awareness of involvement opportunities available.

Because continued learning is a "do-it-yourself" undertaking, several articles have been included on building your own resources. We have specifically dealt with sources for hard copy, pamphlets, charts, publications, abstracts, summaries, etc. As a professional, you must be aware of where to secure information and where to go for reference help. Information about libraries and reference sources is also included. Read on and then add to your own plan for personal growth.

PROFESSIONAL ORGANIZATIONS

Affiliating with professional associations is one reward of having attained a degree. In some cases, it is a ticket to success in your career ladder. The home economics profession is used here as an example in terms of professional affiliations. You will want to explore the opportunities for affiliation in the field of your choice. Most home economists will join at least one professional association while some will affiliate with a general home economics association as well as one or more associations related to their specific area of expertise. Whatever the case, the cost is offset by the benefits gained. (Incidentally, professional memberships are tax deductible.) While you can gain from journals or other materials made available by membership in professional associations, try to become a "doing" member at the district, state, or national level of your organization memberships. This may mean participation in workshops, conferences, committees and more.

The *American Home Economics Association* is the one organization that joins all home economists nationally. The 50,000 plus member organization is a strong force in improving the quality of life for all. Headquartered in Washington, D.C., the organization focuses on all areas of home economics, sponsoring workshops, professional publications and conferences. In more recent years, AHEA has become increasingly involved in public affairs in an effort to impact formation of public policy, has increased participation internationally and has established The Center for The Family. The organization is structured to recognize professional and subject-matter interest areas, such as HEIB (Home Economists in Business) and textiles and clothing. AHEA has state counterpart organizations (e.g., Ohio Home Economics Association) and in *some* states and districts national membership automatically makes you a member within your state or district.

Additionally, departments have identified key organizations related to departmental majors as listed below (*not* in order of importance):

Family Relations and Human Development
National Association for Education of Young Children
Ohio Association for Education of Young Children
National Council on Family Relations
Society for Research in Child Development

Home Economics Education
American Vocational Association
—National Association of Vocational Home Economics Teachers
Home Economics Education Association

Home Management and Housing
American Council on Consumer Interests
Electrical Women's Round Table

Human Nutrition and Food Management
American Dietetic Association
American Institute of Nutrition
Institute of Food Technology
National Restaurant Association
Ohio Food Service Executives Association

Textiles and Clothing
American Association of Textile Chemists and Colorists
Costume Society of America

Information regarding any of the above organizations mentioned is available from departmental faculty members.

MORE THAN JUST BOOKS

Information is vital to the professional home economist. The subject matter areas in home economics are so broad and ever-changing that it has **become more important to know where to get accurate, current information** than to follow a hopeless pursuit of storing the information in our brains. Libraries are in the business of storing information and offering services to get the information quickly and efficiently. No longer strictly book closets, libraries are potential sources of professional aid and development for everyone—even you.

Library systems differ in some policies from location to location but offer essentially the same services. Here we are going to discuss Ohio libraries. The general overview of services and policies will help you wherever you are employed, and will serve as a basis for estimating services available in other state systems. There is no substitute for contacting libraries personally and it is hoped that this chapter will suggest useful questions for you to ask when you need library services.

THE PUBLIC LIBRARY

Public libraries are no longer strictly books. They are information resource centers housing books, periodicals, newspapers, government documents, monographs, speeches, motion picture films, filmstrips, records, tapes, slides, photographs, charts, maps, paintings, prints, sculpture, etc. In addition, you can expect to find reading groups, discussion groups, workshops, seminars, lectures, and other programs to help you garner important information to keep you from becoming a still-watered professional.

Each city will have different public library resources. Some have a cooperative system in which libraries share references and materials, making all resources potentially available to you.

The local public library is a rich source of continued learning and you will find this true throughout the country. Consider the impact of the following services on your professional life.

REFERENCES

Unless you have taken courses in library science, grew up in a library or have an amazing amount of good luck, you may go to the library and leave without the information you need. Your reference librarian is your good luck, directing you to the sources you need and helping you organize and isolate your subject to make most efficient use of your research time. The reference librarian also knows the ins and outs of libraries. If the reference librarian in your local library cannot get the information you need, he or she will contact librarians in larger systems. Reference librarians act as connectors between you and information. The "Beginner's Guide to Research" section of this text will help you communicate with the reference librarian.

The reference division of a large library may offer on-line bibliographic information through a computerized information system, generally for a nominal fee.

Many times a visit to the library is not even necessary. Quick questions like, "What salutation is appropriate when you are writing a business letter and do not know the sex of the receiver?" can be answered by telephone.

Check your local library. For those of you interested in marketing, business, or job hunting, the public library keeps a collection of up-to-date director-ies of corporate addresses, officers, financial history, transfer agents, corporation affiliations, plant locations, sales volumes and products. This information is indexed by name, geographic location, or by products. Investment advisory sources, international trade, financial newspapers and handbooks are also available. These resources are useful in the areas of marketing, family financial counseling, etc., not to mention useful sources of information for job-finding contacts.

AUDIO-VISUAL RESOURCES

One role of a home economist is educating the public. The library can provide audio-visual materials on a wide range of topics. There are rooms and equipment available for previewing materials to help make sure you are getting the right materials for your needs. Some libraries even have a video-tape studio available for use by non-profit community organizations. The cost is minimal.

CHILDREN'S PROGRAMS

Most libraries have good collections of children's literature. Sometimes there are professional staff members available who are able to recommend materials for children who have special needs, children with learning difficulties, or gifted children.

EDUCATIONAL PROGRAMS

Libraries also have informal public education programs. Many times workshops are held in special interest areas. They are a good way to strengthen a weak area. You may even be able to conduct workshops in areas in which you see unmet needs.

Each library has a special emphasis and special services. It is a good idea to ask for a tour of your local library soon after moving to a new city. You need to know what options and resources are available for your per-sonal growth. If your local library resources and services are limited, ask what services are available through interlibrary loan and interlibrary cooperative services.

THE STATE LIBRARY

A State Library, generally located in the state capital, is established to provide information and reading to legislators and state officials. Through the years, the services have evolved to three main functions:

1. Extensive reference and research services.
2. Backup lending system to public libraries throughout the state.
3. Agency for granting federal money to improve library services throughout the state.

Many people are not aware that a State Library serves individual citizens also, and often overlook the extensive services it can provide.

RESOURCES

Because a State Library functions to provide state agencies and employees with information they need to serve the public efficiently, a wide range of resources is available, which are especially valuable to you whatever your interests are.

There are countless books in the State Library available for loan to any citizen. Though you will not find fiction or recent humanities, you will find a wide-ranging collection of social science and technical information. Holdings under divisions of administrative services, urban development, education, health, mental health, and social welfare are particularly useful to the professional. To secure a recent acquisitions list, write to the office of:

Special Services to State Government
The State Library in your state capital

The library also has an extensive collection of periodicals, monographs, papers and other documents in related areas. If a book, periodical or other document is not available from your local library, you may find it worthwhile to check the State Library. The demand for State Library holdings is not as great as the demand for those in a Public or University Library system.

REFERENCES

The State Library limits extensive reference and research services to respond to government officials and state agencies, but the staff will respond to short answer requests from the general public. Some examples of these requests are: verifications of spellings, names of state and federal government officials, and census statistics. Make requests in person, by telephone, or by mail. Using this service can save you time if you need to contact government officials regarding public policy. The staff will research questions referred by your local librarian. Through the local librarian you do have access to the more extensive research services offered by the library.

Another reference service available to persons visiting a State Library is use of the New York Times Information Bank. This is a computerized index that provides bibliographic references from New York Times and over eighty other major newspapers and periodicals on current affairs topics. For instance, you could obtain a bibliography dealing with laetrile, specific legislation, movements, etc. Library computer terminals are available for public use, giving bibliographic data as well as locations of books or documents in libraries throughout the nation. Print-out information is available from these two sources.

You may be interested in government documents for current information in your field. A State Library is a federal depository for these resources. Titles for government documents are found in the *Monthly Catalog for U.S. Government Publications*. Those catalog entries marked with an asterisk(*) are in the State Library. After reading the document, you may decide to order it from the Superintendent of Documents. The librarian will give you the procedure for doing this.

If you find yourself working in an isolated or rural area, you can still use library resources. One way is through your local library. If materials you need are not available from your local library, the librarian can secure them from a State Library which acts as a backup system for all libraries in the state. Bookmobile services are also available in many counties to link you with State Library resources you need. If you are interested in your family history, the library also has a Genealogy Collection and Procedures Division.

STATE LIBRARY POLICIES

Any citizen may use the State Library. However, when you visit the State Library you will find a "closed stacks" system rather than the "open stacks" system used at many universities. To get a book in the closed stack system, you search the card catalog for the book you need. You then fill out a slip to present to the person at the circulation desk. This person retrieves the book for you. The State Library may use the Dewey classification system rather than the Library of Congress classification used at many universities.

UNIVERSITY LIBRARIES

University libraries can be a valuable resource for continued learning. By calling the director of public services or the director of the library, you will be able to find out what services are available to the general public. Usually, any state citizen can secure a courtesy card for use at a state university library. Policies vary widely in private university libraries. Again, call and find out. Many times, even if a private university library does not lend books, books can be used in the library.

ON THE TRAIL OF AN ANSWER
RESEARCH GUIDE

Whether to complete a thesis, answer a client's question, or to prepare court testimony, research is necessary to a professional who must know quick and efficient routes to take in search of a certain answer. This article briefly describes where to start in your search.

Locating the information and publications necessary to answer your questions can be tricky without the help of a reference librarian. Other ways of locating materials are through electronic search systems and through specialized library publications.

For location of books and materials consult the Card Catalog. Some libraries have electronic search systems. Ask the reference librarian for the best route to take. Many times, when materials are not available in one library, the librarian can get them for you through some other library. If you have questions, don't give up — ask.

The *National Union Catalog* and *Union List of Serials* are sources to check for libraries owning desired materials. For instance, if you wanted to see where the closest copy of Comb's *Helping Relationships* was located, look this title up in the *National Union Catalog* and it will tell you who has copies.

The LCS system at OSU is an electronic catalog system that is gradually replacing the card catalog. Information about book locations and holdings, and whether or not the book is checked out within a particular library is available at a glance. To use the LCS system for a subject search, try the LCS Shelflist Placement Search for a list of books on your topic.

If you are having a difficult time finding key words to describe your topic, consult the *Subject Heading Book*. In most libraries, this reference would be located near the card catalog or in the reference department.

Computerized literature searches (like OSU's Mechanized Information Center) are a quick, efficient way to gather references on a given topic. Again, consult your reference librarian for these services. The librarian will tell you where to obtain these services. Cost for these searches varies, depending upon computer time used. Commercial searches of specialized services are also available. Examples are: DATRIX—Direct Access to Reference Information from Xerox which searches Dissertation Abstracts International, or for government research, a NTIS—National Technical Information Service is useful.

The remaining section is a glossary of principal research materials. Definitions of the type of research material is given along with examples of each. The list is only a start!

- *Bibliographies:* a list of books or other materials by an author, on a subject, printed by one printer, in one place, or during one period, and possibly housed in one location. Examples: *Bibliography of Bibliographies, Bibliography Index, International Bibliography of the Social Sciences.*
- *Indexes and Abstracts:* Indexes—to books, magazines, microfiche, newspapers, films, etc. Some indexes are specialized types such as poetry

indexes, documents, military literature, law. Others cover several types of publications. Examples: *Public Affairs Information Service* (PAIS) —to books, pamphlets, articles, documents; *Learning Directory* to multimedia education materials. Abstracts are publication or article summaries including bibliographic referencs to the original. Examples: *Book Review Digest, Dissertation Abstracts International, U.S. Patent Gazette, Chemical Abstracts, Sociological Abstracts, Nutrition Abstracts.*

- *Current Information Tools:* File current events reported in newspapers and magazines. Examples: *Facts on File, Deadline Data on World Affairs, Moody's Industrial Survey, Environment Reporter, Congressional Quarterly Weekly Report.*

  Yearbooks and Almanacs are other sources of current information tools. General examples: *World Almanac, Britannica Book of the Year;* specialized types such as *The Nautical Almanac, Yearbook of International Organizations.*

- *Dictionaries, Encyclopedias, Handbooks:* Etymological dictionaries provide a history of words, a foreign language, or a subject and are listed in the card catalog under title or subject (Dictionaries). *Encyclopedias* hold general information and information in subject areas such as *Encyclopedia of Philosophy. Handbooks* contain miscellaneous facts and figures on one or many subjects assembled for ready use. Examples: AHEA's *Metric Usage Handbook.*

- *Geographical Tools: Atlases and gazeteers* (dictionaries of geographical names are located in reference areas or a map room.

- *Government Documents:* Government publications are usually categorized according to subject area. See the card catalog for these examples: U.S. Laws, *Code of Federal Regulations, Index Medicus, Research in Education,* census reports, *Congressional Record,* Department of Agriculture series, *Statistical Abstract of the United States.* To locate documents, use the *Monthly Catalog of Government Publications,* or the *United Nations Documents Index,* or reference librarians.

- *The In-Print Lists* give information about publishers, prices, addresses, books, paperbacks, microforms, copyrights, etc.

- *Directories* are a list of persons or organizations, systematically arranged, usually in alphabetical or classified order, giving address, affiliations, etc. for individuals and addresses, officers, functions and similar data for organizations. Types of directories are: phone, business information, associations, research centers, hospitals, press, academic world, manufacturers.

- *Biographical Sources:* Consult current figure sample listings — *Who's Who* for certain countries and occupations; *Biography Index* listing articles and books on a person; *American Men and Women of Science.* For retrospective listing, examples are: biographical dictionaries, *New York Times Obituaries Index, Who Was Who.*

Adapted from *A Guide to Library Sources and Services for the Beginning Researcher,* by Nancy J. Keller, Reference Librarian and C. Grey Austin, Honors Director, The Ohio State University, February 1974.

ABSTRACTING

Abstracts are convenient condensations of original papers and research. They serve the two purposes of helping the research worker, educator, student or professional have access to accumulated knowledge in the field and for helping to keep up with new developments in the profession. Abstracts are another way to continue learning. Abstracts differ from indexes and bibliographies which give only titles, references or titles and annotations in that abstracts give the gist of the entire article. Abstracts are usually not over 200 words in length and should include the purpose of the article, important facts in the content and conclusions drawn by the author. An abstract covering a research article should include variables studied, number and type of subjects, description of procedures and a synopsis of the major findings. Abstracts are an efficient means of "keeping up" for professionals. Sometimes one finds abstracts of current research in professional journals, abstract services, dissertation abstracts, or one's own abstracts from reviewed literature.

An abstract is a *non-critical* condensation of a research report or journal article. It should give the reader a clear idea of the content and a basis for deciding whether or not to read the original literature.

Here is a checklist of what should be included in your abstract:

Bibliographic information
_____ author
_____ title
_____ reference to source
_____ date

Body of the work
_____ purpose of the article
or variables studied
_____ important facts on content
(or number and type of subject
and description of procedures)
_____ conclusions of author

GUIDELINES FOR PREPARING ABSTRACTS

1. Read the entire article before starting to write the abstract. Read analytically.
2. Read footnotes as carefully as the main text.
3. Use summaries, tabulation, conclusions, section and chapter headings only as aids in constructing the abstract.
4. Retain the "proportion, mood and tone of the original" as well as possible.
5. Use your own words, though some quotation is permissible. An abstract has, after all, literary qualities of its own and should stand on its own merits as a composition.
6. Use complete sentences avoiding telegraphic style. Short sentences are, in general, preferable to long ones.

7. Avoid types of phrases and words which do not contribute directly to the purpose of the abstract, namely to give the reader condensed information contained in the original. Some usages which abstractors should avoid are spelled out by the Institute of Electrical Engineers, *Science Abstracts: Notes for Guidance of Abstractors* (London). These are: cliches; long words; unnecessary words (however, also, nevertheless); two words where one will do; introductions (In recent years, the subject . . . ; In the present paper, the author . . . ; This article, the first of a series, deals mainly with . . . ; In an appendix . . .).

8. Condensation, hence conciseness, is of course the chief object in abstracting — to save the time of the reader and printing space. Usefulness to the user is a chief determinant as to length of the abstract. More detailed abstracting becomes necessary when the original report is not readily accessible to many research workers or other users. Length of the abstract will obviously be influenced by the kind and volume of the material abstracted. Some abstract specialists state a desirable length of an abstract as *one-third* to *one-fourth* of the original writing; others, 120 to 200 words. One typewritten page is usually sufficient.

9. Abstracts should be objective and impersonal, informative rather than critical. "As space is not available in abstracting journals for authors to reply to abstractors, it is, at the very least, unfair to adopt a critical style. Users of abstracts realize that the opinions expressed are those of the authors, and no stigma is attached to an abstractor for repeating any statements from the original." (*Handbook of Special Librarianship and Information Work,* Wilfred Ashworth, general editor, 1955).

10. All figures and formulas used should be checked and rechecked for accuracy by the abstractor.

11. Once the abstract is committed to paper it should be read and reread, to determine if it accurately reflects the intent of the article.

12. An abstract follows as an example of one type of format to follow.

Journal of the American Dietetic Association
August, 1974, Volume 65
pp. 155-160
E. Ream, E. Wilcox, R. Taylor, J. Bennett
"Tenderness of Beef Roasts"

Subjective and objective tests were applied to study the effect of microwave and conventional cooking on palatability and mineral content of arm and rib roasts. Flavor, juiciness and tenderness were evaluated by a taste panel. Objective tests included the Warner-Bratzler Shear Test for tenderness, hydraulic press for juiciness, evaporation and total cooking loss.

It was found that, overall, the conventional method was more desirable. In general, beef cooked in the microwave was less tender, juicy and flavorful, according to the taste panel, and had higher cooking losses.

Chemical analysis of cooked meat of arm roasts indicated lower tenderness with meat having the highest iron and magnesium content. An increase in juiciness and tenderness were associated with a high sodium content. Meat containing a higher potassium and phosphorus value had less flavor and tenderness. An increase in percentage of lipids was positively correlated with low iron and potassium and high sodium content. Tenderness increased with an increase in lipid content.

YOU AND FAIR USE
The 1976 copyright law

In the course of their work, many professional people routinely make duplications of information for use in their work. These copies are sometimes used as replacements or supplements for instructional materials in some type of teaching situation or they are used to answer a question or concern of a client. As of January 1, 1978, professionals who routinely copy the work of others may also routinely appear in court.

The biggest change in the new law is the doctrine of "fair use." What is fair use? Fair use depends upon these considerations:

— the purpose and character of the use, including whether such use is of a commercial nature or is for nonprofit educational purposes;
— the nature of the copyrighted work;
— the amount and substantiality of the portion used in relation to the copyrighted work as a whole;
— the effect of the use upon the potential market for or value of the copyrighted work.

So what do these considerations mean? In anticipation of this question, Congress supplemented the new law with specific guidelines agreed upon by a committee composed of educators and publishing companies. These guidelines will help you decide what material you can use within the new law.

A USER MAY:

• *Make a single copy* for use in scholarly research, or in teaching a class, of the following:

— a chapter from a book:
— an article from a periodical or newspaper;
— a short story, short essay, or short poem, whether or not from a collected work;
— a chart, graph, diagram, drawing, cartoon, or picture from a book, periodical or newspaper.

• *Make multiple copies* for classroom use only, and not to exceed one per student in a class, of the following:

— a completed poem, if it is less than 250 words and printed on not more than two pages;
— an excerpt from a longer poem, if it is less than 250 words;
— a complete article, story, or essay if it is less than 2,500 words;
— an excerpt from a prose work, if it is less than 1,000 words or 10 per cent of the work, whichever is less;
— one chart, graph, diagram, drawing, cartoon, or picture per book or periodical.

A USER MAY NOT:

• *Make multiple copies* of a work for classroom use if it has already been copies for another class in the same institution.
• *Make multiple copies* of a short poem, article, story, or essay from the same author more than once in a class term, or make multiple copies

from the same collective work or periodical issue more than three times a term.

- *Make multiple copies* of works more than nine times in the same class term.
- *Make a copy* of works to take the place of an anthology.
- *Make a copy* of "consumable" materials, such as workbooks.

In general, any copying of an original work that interferes with the profits of its creator is most likely taboo.

WHEN TO SEEK PERMISSION:

If the use for which you need to make copies of an original does not comply with the guidelines for fair use given here, you should seek copyright permission.

In review of the principles of fair use, photocopying or duplicating by an individual for his or her own use, as long as it is a single copy of an article, short poem or small portion of the work as a whole, is generally considered fair. This covers the copying you occasionally do of information from libraries.

Systematic duplication, whether making multiple copies at one time or single copies that in the aggregate add up to multiple ones, is beyond the boundaries of "fair use." For instance, if you were a consultant who consistently duplicated a magazine article or some other reference and gave it out to the public, you would be violating fair use. *(The fact that a duplication is for a non-profit use has no bearing on the question of fair use.)*

The systematic exchange of photocopies of copyrighted articles that serve as a substitute for purchasing more subscriptions is beyond bounds of fair use. Remember, you cannot interfere with the profits of the originator.

HOW TO SEEK PERMISSION:

Request copyright permission from the publisher. The information you need about copyright for a particular work is on the title page or the reverse side of the title page for that work. After you have determined who owns the copyright, the next step is to write the owner (usually the publisher) for permission to duplicate. You will avoid a lot of delay if you send complete and accurate information in your copyright request. Include:

- — title, author and/or editor, and edition of materials to be duplicated;
- — exact material to be used, giving amount, page numbers, chapters and if possible, a photocopy of the material;
- — number of copies to be made;
- — use to be made of duplicated materials.
- — form of distribution (classroom, newsletter, etc.);
- — whether or not the material is to be sold;
- — type of reprint (ditto, photocopy offset, typeset).

Along with your request, send a copy of the request for the publisher's files, a copy of the material, and a self-addressed, stamped return envelope. Allow plenty of time; granting permission is not always a "yes" or "no" matter. If you have several requests, send them together. Do not ask for blanket permission to duplicate works—it cannot be granted in most cases. In your letter, include a space for any conditions the publisher may have for the use of the duplication.

Writing for copyright material is not complicated and can be treated almost like a form letter. Given its relative ease, permissions seeking should not be a stumbling block. Thus, in addition to the legal conditions set forth in the 1976 law, the professional has ethical considerations about using another's work without credit or permission.

... CONTINUED LEARNING ......
GRADUATE SCHOOL

The need for professionals with advanced degrees is great. In the 1970's, master's degrees were awarded at a ratio of 1 to 9 baccalaureate degrees and doctorates were produced at a ratio of 1 to 131 baccalaureate degrees. You may wish to become one of the "rare" ones and increase your opportunities with an advanced degree. In your search for a job, you have probably come across several positions requiring a graduate degree. Opportunities exist in administration, teaching and research in colleges and universities as well as positions in business, government, and social agencies for highly qualified professionals. Advanced degrees can be advantageous in countless other areas as well.

The reasons for considering graduate school are varied. Persons with higher educational degrees usually command somewhat higher salaries than do those with bachelor's degrees. Many undergraduates feel that they have only an introduction to their field and desire the greater specialization of graduate school. Sometimes this specialization can be developed on the job. Some students in the past have chosen to go to graduate school to avoid the draft or other responsibility. Unfortunately, graduate schools may serve a custodial function for some today as a halfway house between school and the work world. This section deals with common questions prospective graduate students struggle with about graduate school.

1. **Should** I go to graduate school?

Hard questions first! There are many reasons for deciding one way or the other about attending graduate school. Some, of course, are better than others. Mentally list your own reasons and then compare them with the "good" and "not-so-good" categories we have here.

NOT-SO-GOOD
- can't find a job; undecided about career, or similar reasons related to custodial function
- to please family and friends
- afraid to take responsibility for a job in the real world
- status, prestige

GOOD
- to achieve career goals
- desiring to enter a field requiring academic specialization
- to develop critical, analytical thinking skills
- develop leadership and potential for college teaching
- curiosity about a field you really love

Personal characteristics influence your decision to go or not to go to graduate school. Individuals need to be able to work independently to succeed in graduate school. Does it upset you when you are assigned a broad, undefined project? Do you want to know exactly what is expected of you or do you like to plan your own activities and set your own goals?

Graduate study is a sacrifice in many ways. At times graduate students feel they haven't enough time, energy or money. Do you see your need for an advanced degree in light of your personal and professional goals important enough to sacrifice the needed time, energy and money?

Graduate school requires independent thinking. Are you able to express your thoughts and ideas logically, orally, and in writing? Of course, you will develop writing and expressive skills during your graduate studies, but it is a great asset to have these skills from the beginning.

Graduate school requires concentrated periods of study. Are you curious enough or interested enough in your prospective field to stay with a problem until you solve it? Do you enjoy mental gymnastics? Does it bother you to never quite finish a problem?

Entrance requirements vary among graduate institutions. Secure these requirements by writing the admissions office of the college of your interest. The Ohio State University requires a baccalaureate or professional degree from an approved college or university with an educational background in areas that will enable the student to pursue graduate work in the department of specialization, and a 2.7 cumulative point hour ratio (based on a 4.0 scale) for all previous undergraduate work. An applicant with less than a 2.7 cumulative point hour ratio must take the Graduate Record Examination.

Most colleges and universities will consider scores made on the Graduate Record Examination as evidence of eligibility for graduate study. These examinations are scheduled through the United States in January, February, April, June, October and December. Pre-registration is required several weeks in advance and a fee is charged. Additional information such as fee charges, examination locations and dates can be requested from the Educational Testing Service at one of the following addresses:

Box 955
Princeton, New Jersey 08540

1947 Center Street
Berkeley, California 94704

960 Grove Street
Evanston, Illinois 60201

A Minority Graduate Student Locator Service is offered by the Graduate Record Examinations Board. Through this free service, college juniors, seniors and graduates who are members of racial and ethnic minorities in the United States may make their names available to graduate schools seeking minority applicants. To sign up, students complete the registration form contained in the *Information Bulletin* for the Locator Service and the Graduate Record Examination or write:

Minority Graduate Student Locator Service
Box 2615
Princeton, New Jersey 08541

2. **When** should I go to graduate school? Now or later?

This is another one of those questions for which it is helpful to compare thoughts.

IN FAVOR OF NOW
- into the swing of learning, the routine of taking notes, studying, taking exams
- less knowledge to catch up
- may have fewer responsibilities, i.e., family, financial, job
- may be able to command higher salaried or better job once degree is completed
- some jobs require the additional specialization of a graduate degree

IN FAVOR OF LATER
- may find an interest through experience; many students do not know what they want to do with their lives upon receiving their undergraduate degrees
- increased maturity and experience may put new perspective on value of learning
- may get more out of program with insight because of experience
- change of pace, fresher approach to learning
- time to acquire finances to support graduate education

3. **Where** should I go to graduate school?

It is recommended that you choose the best graduate school that you can afford. The "best" school is one noted for graduate education in your particular area of interest. To find out which school is the best for you, you can:

Talk to Professors. Where did your best professors get their graduate degrees? Because of their professional associations, your professors know schools that are strong in your area of interest and can probably tell you whom to contact at certain universities for more information. Your professors will also help you compare various programs and give you an idea of what to expect in graduate school.

Read Professional Journals and Publications. Have you done any library research lately? What names kept popping up in the area of your interest? Professional journals can tell you who is publishing what and where. From what source are the good books in the field coming?

Read Graduate School Bulletins. Check graduate school bulletins and course catalogues for information about specific course work, fees, requirements, names of people, etc. These bulletins are available in the library or can be obtained by writing directly to a school in which you are interested.

Talk to Graduate Students. Talk to graduate students who have experience in a variety of programs. How did they choose a graduate school? What is their program like? What practical wisdom can they impart to you as a prospective graduate student?

Write Letters. Write to schools in which you are interested. Request literature and information about their programs.

Visit Schools. If at all possible, visit prospective schools. Talk to faculty members, students and officials. Do you like the school's facilities, equipment, and the people with whom you will work? Could you be happy in the location? You can find out vital information, firsthand, with a visit.

Compare Schools. Consider the nature of the course offerings, requirements, cost and size of the graduate school. Where are the graduates placed? Consider the number and reputations of the graduate faculty.

It is generally better to do graduate work at institutions other than the one in which you earned your undergraduate degree. This advice may not apply if you are planning to do your graduate work in a different college of the same university.

4. **How** can I finance graduate study?

Graduate school is an investment. If you are planning to attend an out-of-state institution, the costs are even greater. There are several options open to you for financial assistance.

Let the personnel in your prospective department know that you need financial support. Most departments employ a select number of graduates as research, teaching, and/or administrative associates. Sometimes these are called "assistants." These associateships or assistantships require that the student work a specified number of graduate credit hours. Students earn a stipend for this work and sometimes fees may be paid by the university. Fellowships are monetary grants that do not require work in addition to study. These are usually awarded through private agencies, but some are available through government or special university projects. Someone in your department will be able to tell you what is available. Be sure to find out the deadline for submitting applications for associateships or fellowships.

Of course, some students work part-time at other jobs while going to school. Master's degrees usually require a minimum of one year, Ph.D.'s a minimum of three years beyond the Master's. Combining study with work is likely to prolong the time needed to complete your degree.

Be sure to indicate on admissions forms that you wish to be considered for financial support. Visit the financial aids office at your prospective university. Ask what is available in the way of student educational loans, work-study programs, scholarships and fellowships.

5. **Is it possible** to complete a graduate degree in a subject matter area other than the one in which the bachelor's degree is taken?

Yes. As your career goals evolve, a change in academic preparation may be warranted. One becomes more specialized through graduate education. This specialization may take place in either the same or related discipline. Students who choose to change disciplines are usually expected to take some undergraduate coursework in that area to prepare them for graduate work. This work does not count toward the graduate degree. As you would expect, the more closely related the undergraduate field of study is to the graduate field of study, the less make-up work will be required. Your prospective department will specify the amount of work required to make up for background deficits.

Prepared in consultation with:
Dr. Jean D. Dickerscheid
Chairperson, School of Home Economics Graduate Committee
The Ohio State University

ACTIVE

Home economists' responsibility for shaping public policy is inseparable from the mission of home economics—improving the quality of life. Involvement in public policy will make home economists *active* agents for the cause of improving living conditions, rather than *passive* recipients or implementors of government policy.

Although a sophisticated understanding of the legislative process and a passionate involvement in the process is the summit of our hopes for the home economics graduates of The Ohio State University, we realize that the mystery and the "bother" surrounding legislative action keeps most home economists passive. Some are not interested. The following information will hopefully uncover the mystery and give you ideas for minimizing the bother.*

Options for Involvement

You, as a home economist, as well as any other citizen, can be active in the legislative process at many levels. You can choose to become involved as an individual or as part of a group. Think of your concerns and how you can effect change when change is necessary at these levels. . . .

1. **You Can Vote:** Only about one-half of the people registered to vote in national elections do so. Do you? Requirements for voters are that you be:

☐ a U.S. citizen
☐ 18 years old by election day
☐ a resident of the county or precinct 30 days
   (this may vary from state to state)
☐ registered, if required in your area

If you have questions about whether or not you are eligible to vote, call your local County Board of Elections for information. The County Board of Elections will also be able to explain absentee voting policy, if you need to vote in this way. Some counties will send out clerks to register disabled persons. Check before becoming a "no-voter."

2. **You Can Contact Legislators to Express Your Viewpoint**
When contacting legislators, make sure you are contacting the correct level. In other words, do not contact your state legislator about national legislation. This can be done by letter, telegram, mailgram or telephone call. Letters are a very good way to express your viewpoint. State your concern, and support it with documentation. Suggestions for writing letters, prepared by the League of Women Voters, have been included in

---

*The State of Ohio is used as an example in this course manual. Other states have similar structures. To learn exactly how legislative ipolicy works in other states, call the State Capitol Building and ask for the Secretary of State's Office. This office will refer you to the people who can tell you what you need to know.

your manual to help you write effective letters. Though the guidelines will help you write letters that will not reflect negatively upon your profession, they are not cardinal rules. The important thing is to let your legislator know how you feel—in your own words.

As a home economist, you will have specific reasons for opposing or supporting a bill. State these in your letter. Include newspaper or periodical articles and other documentation to support your case. Does the bill interfere with your work effectiveness? Does it violate your moral values? If so, on what grounds? Why do you think the bill will improve the quality of life for the family? For the individual? How will the bill affect your area of expertise? What public good will this bill serve? If you can evaluate proposed legislation in light of these and other questions, you'll soon see that you do have something to write about.

Mailgrams and telegrams are quick, brief ways of reaching your legislator. You will be limited in space for supporting your argument, but each will let your legislator know how you, as a constituent and voter, stand on an issue.

A telephone call is a useful means for contacting legislators. The telephone number can be obtained by contacting the Secretary of State's office or by getting the roster of the Senate and House. In Ohio, this roster is available from the Bill Room at the State House. Remember, your legislator is short on time so do not overuse telephone time.

It is *not* necessary to contact a legislator to find out the status of a bill. Instead, call the Public Information Officer. In Ohio, the number to call is (614) 466-8842 in Columbus, and (800) 282-0253 outside Columbus.

3. You Can Become Involved in Group Action

One contact will not change the destiny of legislation, governmentally speaking, but many contacts to legislators about the same issue can. Group action can be a very effective means of influencing public policy. Working with a group gives you opportunity to pool resources, information, and personnel to affect legislation. Of course, becoming involved in legislation as part of a group means that you may sometimes be required to submit your personal stand on an issue to that of the group. Determine special interest groups concerned with the same issue you are. Know both sides of the issue and why the group takes the stand it does. Your American Home Economics Association public affairs coordinator will have this information for you. Some state associations have public affairs coordinators. If not, find out who is testifying for or against the bill. Special interest groups most likely supply this testimony. Home economists share interests with other organizations. Find out who these are and form coalitions. For instance, home economists could join with the Ohio Commission on Aging to work on legislation concerning the aging.

4. You Can Testify at Public Hearings.

Me, before a senate committee?!! As a home economist, you are qualified to testify as an expert on many issues. Read the "Case for the Late Mrs. Smith" in this chapter. It is important to know the protocol and procedures for testimony. Contact the Public Affairs Coordinator for the Ohio Home Economics Association,* or your AHEA public affairs representative if you will be living in another state. Going through a coordinator will save you a lot of time and may make the difference in your effective or ineffective testimony. Your coordinator acts as your eyes and ears at the State House. She knows who is on the committee to hear your testimony and what kinds of questions they ask. Announcements of public hearings are printed in the Sunday *Columbus Dispatch* (a local newspaper) and in other major newspapers; however, they are always changing. Your coordinator will know when these changes occur and will be able to notify you of these changes. In Ohio, if you choose to testify independently, you can find out time and place of hearings by calling the toll-free number (800) 282-0253, or the legislative information number (614) 466-8842.

5. You Can Share Information

Home economists are in a unique position to educate the public. You can influence public policy by getting others concerned. Share what you know about current legislation with the people with whom you come in contact. Alert them to issues that concern them. Show them how to become involved themselves. Many times, public television or radio stations will give time to nonprofit organizations. You can sometimes use this medium for sharing information. You may choose to share information in a newsletter. Be creative about the ways you can get others involved. AHEA and many state associations like the Ohio Home Economics Association send out newsletters to alert members to specific legislation.

How to Seek Information

How do I know what is going on in legislation? Keeping generally informed through the news media is one way to know some things going on in government. For more specific information, read the announcements of public hearings printed in the newspaper. You can also subscribe to any number of news bulletins put out by special interest groups or professional organizations. OHEA's "Public Affairs Speak Out" is available to members for a nominal charge for four issues. AHEA also publishes a legislative bulletin concerned with policy at the national level. Your state representative to AHEA can provide you with the subscription information. Libraries often keep copies of legislative bulletins from special interest groups on file. In Ohio, up to three free copies of any bill can be obtained from the House or Senate Bill Room, Statehouse, Columbus, Ohio 43215.

Before getting involved in public policy, you should understand the process. The Ohio Citizens' Council has prepared a pamphlet explaining the process in "How a Bill Becomes a Law." Read this and then decide where you can become involved.

---

*Public Affairs Coordinator, OHEA, since 1976 is Marlisa K. Lantz.

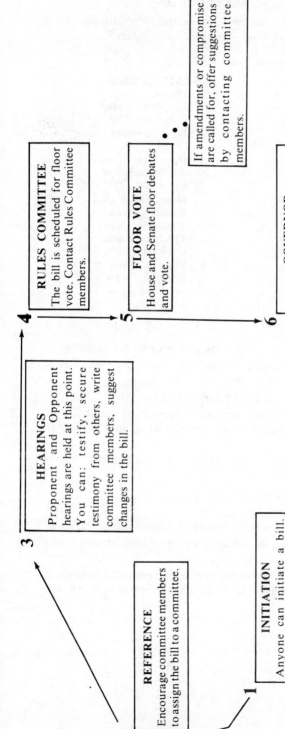

RULES COMMITTEE
The bill is scheduled for floor vote. Contact Rules Committee members.

FLOOR VOTE
House and Senate floor debates and vote.

If amendments or compromise are called for, offer suggestions by contacting committee members.

GOVERNOR
"Babysit" your bill. Do not give up your campaign just because the bill has reached the governor. Contact the governor about your position.

HEARINGS
Proponent and Opponent hearings are held at this point. You can: testify, secure testimony from others, write committee members, suggest changes in the bill.

REFERENCE
Encourage committee members to assign the bill to a committee.

INITIATION
Anyone can initiate a bill. You can research an issue and then write a bill. Find a sponsor in the House or Senate. The sponsor will introduce the bill for you.

What You Can Do & When (legislatively speaking)

Tips on Writing Elected Officials

Elected officials are interested in the opinions of their constituents. Each letter represents a potential vote. What you think does count!

1. Always address your letters correctly:

FEDERAL	**STATE** (of Ohio)
The President The White House Washington, D.C. 20500	The Governor The State House Columbus, Ohio 43215
Dear Mr. President: Very respectfully yours,	Dear Governor (Name): Sincerely yours,
The Honorable (Senator's Name) United States Senate Washington, D.C. 20510	Honorable (Senator's Name) The State House Columbus, Ohio 43215
Dear Senator (Name): Sincerely yours,	Dear Senator (Name): Sincerely yours,
The Honorable (Name) U.S. House of Representatives Washington, D.C. 20515	Honorable (Name) The State House Columbus, Ohio 43215
Dear Mr. (Name): Sincerely yours,	Dear Mr. (Name): Sincerely yours,

2. Remember to always use your own words and your own stationery.
3. It is perfectly acceptable to send a handwritten letter, as long as it is legible.
4. Keep your letter brief and state your point clearly.
5. Always identify the bill to which you are referring by number and description. Remember to state why you are interested in a particular bill.
6. Don't send carbon copies to several officials. Write each one individually.
7. Remember to be courteous and reasonable.
8. Never threaten or harass a legislator.
9. Include editorials or articles from periodicals if they support your case.
10. Remember to say thank you if he or she does something of which you approve.
11. It is perfectly acceptable to communicate with committee members who are holding hearings on a bill that interests you, even if you are not in their district.
12. WRITE TODAY

In order to follow the legislative process intelligently, certain words, phrases, and terminology must become a part of the educator's working vocabulary. The following are selected from the materials prepared by the League of Women Voters of the United States, 1739 M St. N.W., Washington, D.C. 20036

Act—technically, the designation of a bill after it has passed one house of Congress. Also used as a synonym for law.

Appropriations Bill—permits the expenditure of monies approved by an authorization bill, but not necessarily to the total permissible under the authorizing legislation.

Authorization Bill—legislation setting up or continuing programs; sets general aims and purposes and may set a ceiling for funding.

Bill—legislative proposal introduced in either house (until it has been passed by that house). Designated HR (House of Representatives) or S (Senate) according to the house in which it originates and by a number assigned in the order in which it was introduced.

Budget—document sent to Congress by the President in January of each year estimating revenues and expenditures for the ensuing fiscal year.

Calendars—arrangements for scheduling legislative business.
House:
  Union—bills for revenue and appropriations
  House—other public bills
  Private—bills pertaining to individual or private interests
  Consent—controversial bills
  Discharge—motions to discharge from committee
Senate:
  Legislation—all bills
  Executive—items under advise and consent power

Clean Bill—after a committee has considered and revised a bill they may rewrite it, incorporating their amendments into a new or "clean bill."

Closed Rule—(House) prohibits the offering of amendments, thus requiring that the bill be accepted or rejected as reported by committee.

Cloture—a process by which debate can be ended in the Senate. A motion for cloture requires 16 senators' signatures for introduction and the support of two-thirds of those present and voting.

Committee of the Whole—when the House sits as one committee to consider legislation reported by a standing committee before it goes to the floor; the committee debates and amends legislation. Requires only 100 members for a quorum.

Committee Report—written explanation and justification for recommendations. Submitted by committee to full chamber after the committee has scrutinized and decided to report a bill favorably. Used by courts, executive departments, and the public as a source of information on the purpose and meaning of a law.

Conference Committee—a committee made up of members from both houses; purpose is to iron out differences between House and Senate versions of a bill.

Congressional Record—daily record of the proceedings and debates of Senate and House; not always a verbatim account of floor debate.

Motion to Recommit—a motion to send a bill back to committee; used to "kill" or delay a bill.

Open Rule—(House)germane amendments are permitted to be adopted by majority vote of the House.

Pairing—an agreement between members on opposite sides of an issue not to vote on a specific question.

Party Leader—(majority and minority) chief strategist and floor spokesman for his party. Elected by party caucus.

Pigeonhole—shelving a bill without a final vote; usually refers to blockage by a committee; allows a bill to die by failure of a committee to act.

Privileged Bills—(House) bills that have precedence over normal order of business and do not require Rules Committee action; reports from Committee on Appropriations on general appropriations bills, and reports from Committee on Ways and Means on bills raising revenue are privileged bills.

Quorum—number of members who must be present to conduct business; in the House it is 218 and in the Senate it is 51.

Ranking Member—member of a committee who has more seniority on the committee than any other member of his party. Usually used in reference to the most senior minority party member.

Rider—an amendment proposing substantive legislation attached to another bill.

Seniority—refers to length of uninterrupted service in Congress, and specifically on a committee; criterion for determining committee chairmanships.

Session—normally, each Congress consists of two sessions, usually beginning in January and ending when Congress adjourns for the year.

Standing Committee—committee whose existence is permanent and continuing from one Congress to the next; there are 21 in the House and 17 in the Senate.

Subcommittee — smaller subject-matter divisions of a committee; facilitates specialization and division of labor.

Suspension of the Rules—in the House a two-thirds majority may suspend the rules and bring a bill directly to the floor; in the Senate, only a majority vote is needed.

Teller Votes—(House)taken in Committee of the Whole by counting congressmen for or against a measure as they walk down the aisle; (until the Legislative Reorganization Act of 1970, there was no provision for recording teller votes).

Unanimous Consent—usual way of conducting business in the Senate; after morning hours, majority leader asks unanimous consent to consider pending legislation; such requests are rarely objected to; also used in both houses in lieu of a vote on noncontroversial measures.

Veto—action by the President if he doesn't approve a bill; he returns it with his objections to the house of origin and the bill may be reconsidered, but it must receive approval of two-thirds of both chambers to become law.

Whip—chosen by party caucus as an assistant to the floor leader; his job is to keep in touch with all members of his party, discover their voting intentions, and get them to the floor for a vote.

THE CASE OF THE LATE MRS. SMITH, HOMEMAKER:

Preparing Testimony for the Court

by Florence Turnbull Hall

To the bereaved, the death of a family member is an immeasurable loss.

When that person has been wife, mother, and homemaker, the emotional strains on the family can be devastating. But the financial hardship in a family that has lost a woman's work contributions is severe, too—and is often overlooked by those caught up in the tragedy of her death.

In court cases dealing with death or disability, however, this financial issue must be faced. Home economists in family economics or home management are occasionally asked to testify in these cases as expert witnesses.

The number of hours spent by homemakers in household tasks and the current weekly or yearly dollar value of those tasks must figure in the court testimony. The expert witness must calculate the financial loss to the family for some years into the future and then discount this loss to present value. For homemakers who were employed outside the home, the expert witness must also calculate the present value of the loss of her future earnings.

But how are we to arrive at the present value of these financial losses? What is essential is that we draw on economic data from various sources and take a comprehensive approach in our calculations.

In the cases for which I have prepared court testimony, some have involved only the financial loss resulting from the loss of homemaking services; others have involved this loss plus loss of future earnings.

In a recent case involving both kinds of financial loss, the court award for the financial loss to a family as a result of the homemaker's death was $353,000. (This homemaker had planned to return to work as a high school home economics teacher, but was not working outside the home at the time of her death.)

I have prepared sample court testimony for this article to show the financial loss to a family resulting from the death in 1973 of the 32-year-old wife (employed full time), who was the mother of one child. I will call this homemaker Mrs. Smith. In Mrs. Smith's case, the total financial loss to her family on her death would be $355,399. The way of arriving at this figure will be reviewed below.

Factors in Financial Loss

As we have seen, the figures for financial loss because of a homemaker's death vary. They do so because of a wide assortment of factors. It is essential for the home economist as expert witness to take into account the hours the homemaker worked outside the home, her family size, the ages and number of her children, and the current wage rates payable for occupations equivalent to the tasks performed by the homemaker.

In addition, the calculations are affected by her earnings, her husband's earnings, her husband's life expectancy (or her life expectancy if she is younger), the expected rate of increase in future wages or salary, and the expected rate of increase in the cost of living.

Finally, for a complete picture, we compute the proportionate cost of the family consumption that is attributable to her out-of-the-family income after taxes and compute the after-tax interest rate at which we discount future loss to present value.

The Cost of Household Tasks

In my own work, I like to use household-task data gathered in the Seattle area by M.P. Schroeder and myself and which have been reported in a previous issue of the *Journal of Home Economics* (1). A number of other authors

have reported similar data that can be used (2, 3).

In Mrs. Smith's case, she would have been part of a three-person family until 1986 (when her child would be age 22), and then part of a two-person family until 1999 (her husband's life expectancy).

The number of hours per week spent at household tasks by homemakers employed full time outside the home and who are members of two- and three-person families appears in Table 1. Table 2 shows the average hourly and weekly value of household tasks performed by part-time homemakers in two- and three-person families, based on prevailing wage rates. Both tables are based on data collected in the Seattle area.

The Computational Method

1. Using both Table 1 and Table 2, we begin assessing the value of Mary Smith's time as a part-time homemaker in a three-person family, less the cost of her support until her child is age 22 in 1986. (For the derivation of the multipliers in the computational steps that follow, see footnotes.)

Thus, *annual value of time spent on homemaking tasks, 1973-86,* would be:

1974 value: $130.05/week x 52 weeks = $6,763

1973 value, discounted at 5% compound annual wage-growth rate:

$6,763 x .9524 = $6,441

1986 value at 5% compound annual wage-growth rate:

$6,763 x 1.7959 = $12,146

Average annual value, 1973-86:

($6,441 + $12,145) divided by 2 = $9,293

2. The *estimated cost of Mrs. Smith's support, 1973-86, would be:*

Smith family average annual income after federal income and social security taxes, 1971-72: $9,074.

Estimated 1972 cost of Mrs. Smith's support:

$9,074 x .30 = $2,722

1973 cost of support at 3% annual compound price-increase rate:

$$\$2,722 \ x \ 1.03 = \$2,804$$

1986 cost of support at 3© annual compound price-increase rate:

$$\$2,722 \ x \ 1.5126 = \$4,117$$

Average annual cost of support, 1973-86:

$$(\$2,804 + \$4,117) \text{ divided by } 2 = \$3,461$$

3. The *average annual financial loss because of the loss of the home-maker's services, 1973-86,* would be:

$$\$9,293 - \$3,461 = \$5,832$$

4. The *present value of an annuity of $5,832 for 13 years (1973-86) discounted at 5% (after tax), compound annual interest rate,* would be:

$$\$5,832 \ x \ 9.394 = \$54,786$$

5. The *value of Mrs. Smith's time as a part-time homemaker in a two-person family during her husband's life expectancy after their child is 22 (1986-1999)* would be:

Value in 1974:

$$\$92.38/\text{week} \ x \ 52 \text{ weeks} = \$4,804$$

Value in 1986 at 5% per year compound wage-growth rate:

$$\$4,804 \ x \ 1.7959 = \$8,628$$

Value in 1999 at 5% growth rate:

$$\$4,804 \ x \ 3.3864 = \$16,268$$

Average annual value, 1986-99:

$$(\$8,628 + \$16,268) \text{ divided by } 2 = \$12,448$$

6. The *estimated cost of Mrs. Smith's support, 1986-99,* would be:

1972 cost of support (from step 2): $2,722.

1986 cost of support at 3% annual compound price-increase rate:

$$\$2,722 \ x \ 1.5126 = \$4,117$$

1999 cost of support at 3% compound annual rate of price increase:

$$\$2,722 \ x \ 2.2213 = \$6,046$$

Average annual cost of support, 1986-99:

$$(\$4,117 + \$6,046) \text{ divided by } 2 = \$5,082$$

7. The *average annual financial loss because of the loss of homemaking services, 1986-99,* would be:

$$\$12,448 - \$5,082 = \$7,366$$

8. The *1986 value of an annuity of $7,366 for 13 years discounted at 5% (after tax), compound annual interest rate,* would be:

$$\$7,366 \ x \ 9.394 = \$69,196$$

9. The *1974 value of $69,196 in 1986, discounted at 5% (after tax), compound annual interest rate,* would be:

$$\$69,196 \ x \ .5568 = \$38,528$$

10. The *value of Mrs. Smith's earnings, 1973-99* (the end of Mr. Smith's life expectancy period), would be:

1973 earnings rate: $667/month or $8,004/year.

1999 earnings at 5% annual compound wage-growth rate:

$$\$8,004 \times 3.5557 = \$28,460$$

Average annual earnings, 1973-99:

$$(\$8,004 + \$28,460) \text{ divided by } 2 = \$18,232$$

TABLE 1

Average Hours Per Week Devoted to Household Tasks by Homemakers Who Work Outside the Home 40 or More Hours Per Week

Household Tasks	Two-Person Family	Three-Person Family
Meal preparation	8.1	11.0
Dishwashing	3.5	4.5
Laundering	2.4	3.6
Sewing	.7	0.7
House care	6.2	7.8
Yard work	—	0.1
Management and shopping	2.6	3.2
Transportation of others	0.7	1.1
Family care and other	3.7	6.6
Total	27.9	38.6

The data were obtained in the Seattle, Washington area in 1968-69.

Note: Some of the data in this table had previously been reported by the author and M.P. Schroeder in "Effects of Family and Housing Characteristics on Time Spent on Household Tasks," *Journal of Home Economics* 62: 23-29: January 1970.

Further cross tabulations provided data for homemakers who work outside the home 40 or more hours per week and are members of two-person and three- to five-person families, but none for three-person families alone.

Consequently, the hours spent on household tasks on the average by *all* homemakers who worked outside the home 40 or more hours per week are used as a conservative estimate for homemakers in three-person families.

Footnote

In step 1, the multiplier .30 is derived from U.S. Bureau of Labor Statistics table (6) showing that a family with one parent and one child needs 70 per cent of the amount for a family of two parents and one child to maintain the same standard of living.

Compound interest tables, available in libraries and university bookstores, are used to obtain the present and future value multipliers. Although it is easier to use a calculator, it is well to be able to use the interest tables in case one's expertise is challenged.

Three multipliers or compound interest factors used in the computations are explained in detail here for those who may not be familiar with the use of compound interest tables.

In step 1, the multiplier .9524 is the present value of $1 one year in the future (present/future or P/F) at 5 per cent annual compound interest (or growth) rate. In other words, $.9524 placed in the bank today at 5 per cent compound annual interest will grow to $1 in one year.

In some tables, .9524 would be called a discount factor. In one illustration, $1 of 1974 wages is equivalent to $.9524 of 1973 wages because of a 5 per cent compound annual rate of increase in wages.

Also in step 1, the multiplier 1.7959 is the future value, 12 years in the future (1986 - 1974 = 12 years), of $1 in the present (F/P) at 5 per cent annual compound interest (or growth) rate. In other words, $1 placed in the bank today at 5 per cent will grow to $1.7959 in 12 years— or, as in the illustration, $1 of 1974 earnings is equivalent to $1.7959 in 1986 earnings if there is a 5 per cent annual compound rate of growth in earnings.

In step 4, the multiplier 9.394 is the present value of an anuity of $1 per year for 13 years at 5 per cent annual compound interest rate.

Thus, if it takes $9.394 now earning 5 per cent to provide an income of $1 per year for 13 years, it takes $54,786 now ($5,832 multiplied by 9.394) to provide an income of $5,832 per year for 13 years.

When using compound interest tables, the beginner has to be careful to distinguish between present and future value factors for single payments and the present and future value factors for annual payments.

Present value of annuity of $18,232 for 26 years, discounted at 5% (after tax) compound annual interest rate:

$$\$18,232 \ x \ 14.375 = \$262,085$$

11. This summary step totals the *present value of the financial loss to a family from the death of Mrs. Smith, 1973-99,* which would be:

Loss of homemaking services, less the cost of her support, 1973-1986:

$$\$54,786 \text{ (subtotal from step 4)}$$

Loss of homemaking services, less the cost of her support, 1986-1999:

$$\$38,528 \text{ (subtotal from step 9)}$$

Loss of Mrs. Smith's earnings, 1973-1999:

$$\$262,085 \text{ (subtotal from step 10)}$$

Total: $355,399, the sum that Mrs. Smith's family will try to recover in a lawsuit.

TABLE 2

**Average Hourly and Weekly Value of
Household Tasks of Part-Time Homemakers in Two- and Three-Person Families,
Seattle, Washington, 1974**

Equivalent Occupation	*Wage and Salary Rates	Hourly Rate	Value per Week	
			Two-Person Family	Three-Person Family
Cook	$23.08-$29.53/day	$3.29	$29.65	$36.19
Dishwasher	$20.03/day	2.50	8.75	11.25
Launderer	$2.83-$3.95/hour	3.39	8.14	12.20
Seamstress	$3.08-$3.55/hour	3.32	2.32	2.32
Housekeeper	$2.50-$3/hour	2.75	17.05	21.45
Gardener	$2.50-$3/hour	2.75	—	.28
Bookkeeper	$629-$792.50/month	4.08	10.61	13.06
Taxi driver	$2/hr + commissions	2.25	1.58	2.48
Teacher, nurse, other	$758-$866/month (general duty nurse rate)	4.67	17.28	30.82
Total			$92.38 ($3.31/hr)	$130.05 ($3.37/hr)

*Rates for Seattle, Wash. from Wage Analysis Unit of Washington State Employment Security Department, June 6, 1974.

Selection of Data

Data in Tables 1 and 2, as mentioned earlier, were collected in the Seattle area by a colleague and me. Other data used in preparing this testimony are from the Wage Analysis Unit of the state of Washington's Employment Security Department; the U.S. Department of Labor; the Federal Reserve Board; and the Internal Revenue Service.

In most cases, the latest wage rates for the various occupations involving services equivalent to household tasks were obtained by telephone and, as such, have been accepted by the court.

There may be occasions, however, when the expertise of a home economist is challenged in the area of wage rates during cross-examination. The result is that a witness from the Wage Analysis Unit may be called to corroborate the validity of the rates used.

Expected Future Income

For that part of the testimony requiring a projection over *x* years of the estimated wage increases the deceased would have had, I usually use "Gross

Average Hours and Earnings of Production or Nonsupervisory Workers on Private Nonagricultural Payrolls, 1947-1973," published in every issue of the *Monthly Labor Review*. I base the expected rate of wage increase on the rate of increase in the past x years.

The number of years into the future for which wages are to be estimated is determined from information on the family involved. The next step involves going that number of years *backward* in the table in order to obtain average weekly earnings of x years ago. The compound rate of growth in wages is then calculated from the earnings of x years ago and the earnings for the latest year recorded in the table.

For example, when estimating increases for 13 years into the future, go back 13 years in time from the latest year recorded in the table (1973 in the case of Mrs. Smith) and calculate the compound annual rate of increase in wages from 1960 to 1973. This is rounded to the nearest whole number (in this case, 4.58 percent becomes 5 percent).

Compound interest tables can be used as compound rate of growth tables and are useful in the calculation. A calculator programmed for financial calculations makes the task still easier.

In some cases, Bureau of the Census data *(4)* on family and personal income or on income-growth rates may be more suitable than production worker earnings.

The Expected Cost of Support

Family income is important in calculating the cost of support of the deceased. I usually use the family income after taxes for the year preceding the year of death. If family income is above average, a percentage based on annual rates of personal savings may be subtracted in order to arrive at an annual consumption cost for the family *(5)*.

The percentage of net family income or of consumption attributable to the cost of support of the deceased is derived from scale values in the Bureau of Labor Statistics Revised Equivalence Scale *(6)*.

The compound rate of price increase used in estimating cost of support of the deceased in future years is calculated from past "all items" consumer price indexes, again going back in time the same number of years that one is estimating into the future. The *Federal Reserve Bulletin* and the *Monthly Labor Review* are both convenient sources of consumer price indexes for past years.

The Interest Rate

The rate most likely to be challenged in cross-examination is the interest rate used in discounting estimated future value of household services and/or future earnings to present value. Since only part of the court award would be used each year, the remainder would earn interest, thus decreasing the number of dollars needed now to replace the annual loss. The higher the interest rate, the fewer the dollars needed now to replace the annual loss. The higher the interest rate, the fewer the dollars needed now to produce that annual income or future value.

Because recent interest rates have been high, the 5% after-tax rate used in the sample testimony may be questioned. The after-tax interest rate equivalence to the before-tax rate selected depends, of course, on the tax bracket at which the interest is likely to be taxed.

To arrive at an estimate of this tax bracket, project the surviving husband's earnings into future years and calculate his average earnings in dollars over the years he would use the court award in order to replace lost services and income. The interest on the court award, added to his other income, would be taxed at a level at or above the top tax rate on his other earnings. Since the rate of increase in earnings is an estimate, and since income tax exemptions, deductions, and rates change, this is understandably a rough estimate.

Since the before-tax interest rate selected must be one which the plaintiff could reasonably expect to earn safely many years into the future (in Mrs. Smith's case, 26 years), a reasonable choice is the rate on long-term government bonds.

When the calculations used in Mrs. Smith's case were done, the latest yield shown in the *Federal Reserve Bulletin* was 7.07 percent. The estimated average tax rate on the interest from the annuity was 30 percent. Thus, the after-tax interest that the award money could reasonably be expected to earn safely was $7.07 - (.30 \times 7.07) = 4.95\%$ (or 5% rounded).

It is wise to have in mind, when cross-examined, the various means by which one can currently earn higher interest rates and to be prepared to defend the one used.

Conclusion

Clearly, those of us who are called upon to be expert witnesses in court cases of this nature must be both familiar and comfortable with the economic analyses described above. Economists and home economists who specialize in family economics and home management are, of course, likely candidates for this role.

But whether or not we will actually be called upon to testify, the issue affects us all. For women who are homemakers, wage earners, or some combination of both, the figures are not only revealing but are also essential to an understanding of women's role and valuation in contemporary society.

References

1. Hall, F.T., and Schroeder, M.P. "Effects of Family and Housing Characteristics on Time Spent on Household Tasks." *Journal of Home Economics* 62: 23-29; Jan. 1970.
2. Walker, K.E., "Homemaking Still Takes Time." *Journal of Home Economics* 61: 621-624; Oct. 1969.
3. Manning, S.L. *Time Use in Household Tasks by Indiana Families.* Purdue University Agricultural Experiment Station Research Bulletin No. 837, 1968.
4. U.S. Department of Commerce, Bureau of the Census. "Money Income in 1973 of Families and Persons in the United States," in *Current Population Reports: Consumer Income.* Series P-60, No. 93 Washington, D.C. U.S. Government Printing Office, July 1974 (advance report), p. 8. This report is published annually.
5. Federal Reserve Board. "Relation of Gross National Product, National Income and Personal Income and Saving" (indexed under "National Income"). *Federal Reserve Bulletin.* Washington, D.C.: U.S. Government Printing Office, Sept. 1974, p. A57. This report is published monthly.
6. U.S. Department of Labor, Bureau of Labor Statistics. *Revised Equivalence Scale: For Estimating Equivalent Incomes or Budget Cost by Family Type.* Bulletin 1570-2. Washington, D.C.: U.S. Government Printing Office, Nov. 1968, p. 4.

See also

Felmley, J. *Working Women: Homemakers and Volunteers—An Annotated Selected Bibliography.* Washington, D.C.: Business and Professional Women's Foundation, 1975.

CHAPTER 7

A A A ➜➜➜ ATTITUDES
ATTRIBUTES
APPEARANCE

Professionalism is a difficult characteristic to name. These former graduates of the School of Home Economics at The Ohio State University have defined professionalism as they see it in their fields and from their backgrounds. Each has a unique idea to offer, yet a common thread ties them together. Professionalism is personally defined and it is a *process*, not an arrival.

Write your own definition of professionalism and watch it change over the years.

Theresa S. Connor is presently an Assistant Buyer for J.C. Penney Co. in New York.
She graduated in the Combined Bachelor's/Master's Degree program in 1977 with a major in Textiles and Clothing.

"To me, professionalism is my ability to handle myself in my professional position. It is a combination of education and experience for both are important and interrelated. I view professionalism as a growing process where I constantly add to my professional knowledge and outlook."

Rachel D. Warren has been employed by the United Cerebral Palsy Association in the capacities of instructor and program director in Franklin County and as Assistant to Director of Programs and Program Consultant in New York. She earned her B.S. degree in Home Economics at Appalachian State University and has completed her M.S. degree and additional coursework in the School of Home Economics, the area of Home Management and Housing at The Ohio State University.

"Professionalism is a commitment to:
—developmental learning experiences for individuals and families;
—interdisciplinary communications with other professionals;
—legislative activities on behalf of families/communities;
—ongoing acquisition of knowledge and self-improvement;
—adherence to codes of ethics and standards of performance consistent with current philosophies and practices of home economics."

Lynn S. Esselstein, R.D., is Program Director and Nutrition Education Consultant for the Dairy Council of Mid-Ohio. She graduated with a B.S. degree in Home Economics, General Dietetics, from the Ohio State University. She finished her degree in 1977 with emphasis on Nutrition Education.

"Professionalism is that quality inherent in an individual's behavior, not governed by rules or regulations, whereby the individual consistently demonstrates the highest level of poise, maturity, and technical excellence. It is a personally defined philosophy which guides the individual's beliefs, actions, judgments, and decisions."

75

Susan Gregory Jakob is presently director and teacher at the Bexley Methodist Pre-school and previously held a similar position in Oakland, California. Susan also has experience as a substitute teacher in the public schools of Boston and Chicago. She graduated with a Bachelor of Education degree from Northeastern Illinois State University, and an M.S. in Home Economics at The Ohio State University in 1977 in the area of Family Relations and Human Development and is presently a candidate for a doctoral degree here.

Lynda Jenkins Heyl, Springfield, Ohio, is a county extension agent for Clark Co. She graduated with a B.S. in Home Economics, major in Textiles and Clothing and finished her M.S. degree in Textiles and Clothing in Autumn 1978 at The Ohio State University.

Robert C. Hillestad, Ph.D., is a professor in the College of Home Economics at the University of Nebraska. Before beginning his career as a professor, he was a buyer for Marshall Field and Co. and a freelance designer in

"To me a professional is one who goes that extra mile in his/her job in order to better serve humanity. The professional feels that his/her profession makes a difference in people's lives. S/he considers his/her diploma not as an end to education but rather as the beginning of continued growth and development, as s/he creatively explores and implements new ideas in his/her field. S/he is a sterling example to others in his/her profession as s/he grows individually and helps his/her profession to grow."

"Professionalism is a combination of attributes. It is being aware of new developments in one's field, trends in the economy and human behavior relevant to that field. It is being aware of one's career direction, goals and changes, of personal needs and growth, and of the self as an individual. And, it is an awareness of pertinent details, of possible improvements and open-mindedness to change. Professionalism is an understanding of how one's field of specialization relates to other fields, and to families and individuals. It is a personal dedication to and belief in what one is doing. A "professional aura" is the atmosphere surrounding true professionals and is created by blending these personal characteristics: interest, enthusiasm, excitement, distinctive appearance, confidence, control, and an inquisitive, perfecting attitude."

"Professionalism is the practice of structuring one's behavior to meet the needs of others while operating within the framework of some type of involvement which requires specialized education and training."

San Francisco. He obtained his doctorate from The Ohio State University in 1974 in Textiles and Clothing.

Cynthia J. White graduated with her B.S. in Home Economics degree in General Dietetics in 1975 from The Ohio State University. Since that time she has been a nutrition educator for the Ohio Department of Health and is now assistant therapeutic dietition at Grant Hospital.

"A professional person is lucky enough to be able to be paid for performing a skill that he/she enjoys. There is also a fellowship built on common experiences with others in the profession. Responsibility accompanies this honor. There is a responsibility to maintain the highest ethical standards. There is also a responsibility to maintain and increase one's level of skill through peer review, research, and continuing education. Pride implies promoting the contribution made by one's profession. Another professional responsibility and privilege is to support one's Alma Mater and to give help and guidance to those studying the profession. Finally, one must be receptive to potential advances in the profession. In other words, professionalism is sharing and caring."

Joetta W. Cooper of Springfield, Ohio is a Vocational Home Economics Supervisor for Springfield City Schools. She has also taught home economics both as a general home economics teacher and a vocational teacher. She obtained her B.A. in Home Economics degree from Ohio Wesleyan University and is pursuing graduate work in Home Economics Education at The Ohio State University.

"Professionalism means believing that home economics is vitally important and reserving a part of one's life where home economics comes first. (A prerequisite to professionalism is competence in home economics. It is left to the universities to set those standards.) Professionalism includes keeping up-to-date on content, legislation and trends. Decisions must be based on what will advance the cause of home economics. An attempt must always be made to present oneself in such a manner that the association of the person and the field is positive. Support of representative organizations is essential."

Roberta Null, a recipient of a Ph.D. degree in Home Economics at The Ohio State University, has taught home economics on the high school and junior high levels. She is now an Assistant Professor in Housing and Residential Interiors at Purdue University. She earned a B.S. degree in Home Economics at South Dakota State University and an M.A. degree in Home Economics Education at the University of Minnesota.

"To me professionalism means being proud to be a home economist and to present myself, my profession, and my school in the best possible light whenever I can. It means active participation in professional organizations. Attending meetings, serving on committees and other involvement in such organizations as AHEA, Omicron Nu, Phi U and the American Association of Housing Educators have contributed a great deal to both my personal and professional growth. The exchange of ideas and development of friendships through these organizations have been stimulating and fun."

Analie Lynn Wolfe graduated with a B.S. degree in Home Economics in 1975 and has been a buyer for F & R Lazarus for four years. While at The Ohio State University, she was a member of the home economics Honors program in Textiles and Clothing.

"I believe that one's success in a career is directly related to the degree of professionalism attained. Professionalism is not a natural ability but a learned attitude. It develops only within people who believe that their work is an asset to society. To become a professional requires conscious thought and decision-making by an individual on how she/he can most effectively work with people, both in and out of the work environment. Until these decisions are made one can't maintain a professional attitude cognitively and superficially."

Risse Layne McDuffee has been a vocational home economics teacher most of her professional life. She graduated from Berea College with a B.S. degree in Home Economics Education. She obtained her M.S. of Home Economics Education degree at the University of Kentucky and completed her Ph.D. in Home Economics Education at The Ohio State University in August 1978.

"Professionalism is the good feeling one gets following the wise use of one's 'God-quest' talents. It is also that phenomenon that enables a person to achieve a sense of self-worth, to develop a positive self-concept, and to realize self-actualization. When an individual utilizes opportunities or initiates situations to apply his/her knowledge and skills to the service of mankind, then the person is experiencing and manifesting professionalism. Professionalism is an attitude and a dedication which is based on sound principles and an inner code of ethics and

78

motivates one to establish a purposeful living for self and to help others to do the same."

Alice Karen Hite earned her B.S. degree in Home Economics at The Ohio State University majoring in Home Economics Education. She began her career as a home economics instructor and is presently a home economics supervisor at Licking Co. Joint Vocational School.

"Professionalism is a total commitment to all things connected to Home Economics and your current position in the professional world. This includes willingness "to go the extra mile" each day necessary and "to stand up and be counted." One must always have a complete dedication to being totally involved in professional life which calls for a delicate mix of personal life commitments also. Professionals must "do" for themselves and the profession—not wait for someone else to do it."

Patricia Davis, Dayton, Ohio, teaches Home Economics at the high school level. She graduated with a B.S. in Home Economics degree at The Ohio State University.

"Professionalism is following through or putting to use the ethics and ideals of a chosen area for which a person has been trained and educated. When a person chooses a vocation in life, he or she should enter into it with a feeling of pride for the work and a sense of responsibility to uphold the goals and that made it worthwhile and admirable profession."

Rita Rowland Lane, Fairborn, Ohio, graduated in 1974 with a B.S. in Home Economics degree and a major in Home Economics Education. She has taught home economics since graduation and is serving as Acting Vocational Home Economics Supervisor for Springfield City Schools.

"Professionalism involves those qualities I strive for as a home economist. I consider my work as a home economics teacher a career, not merely a job. It is ongoing. It does not end daily at 3:00 or yearly in June. Keeping up to date is a priority for me. I meet this priority by attending inservice workshops, classes at an available university, conference conventions of professional groups and reading on my own. In my work, I constantly set goals for improving my teaching. As I fulfill these, I move on and set new goals. Human relations is an important aspect of teaching. I foster an open relationship with my students. After all, working to change their behaviors is the goal of teaching."

Debby Boch Ireland, Findlay, Ohio, graduated with a B.S. degree in Home Economics, majoring in Family Relations and Human Development, from The Ohio State University. She is a Home Based Specialist with the Blanchard Valley Center in Findlay.

"In my opinion, professionalism is a positive and constructive reflection of the total scope of one's profession. The total scope includes job attitudes and performance, relationships with co-workers, and public image. One must be able to deal with situations objectively and realistically, separating personal from actual fact. Developing and maintaining a professional attitude (professionalism) is a long process— it requires constant nurturing."

Charlette Gallagher, of Columbus, Ohio, is presently Assistant Professor in the Medical Dietetics Division here at The Ohio State University. She graduated with a B.S. degree in Foods and Nutrition from Oklahoma State University and obtained both her degree in Medical Dietetics and her Ph.D. in Human Nutrition at The Ohio State University.

" 'Professionalism' means to me 'the spirit and behavior exemplified by any person, no matter what his/her vocation or avocation, who is dedicated to achieving that which is the highest within his/her grasp'."

TICK, TICK, TICK, TICK, TICK ....

Everyone, but especially professionals, has time demands coming from several directions. Family, friends, job demands, and your community all clamour for your time. How do you juggle it all?

What we value will influence our juggling. You have heard that we have time for those things we truly want to do. Know what you value. It helps to write out the important roles you play and then to put these roles in a hierarchy of importance to you. This is a basis for decision making for what to do and when. Other people influence our time management. Again, know what roles are important to you. Maybe it is time to begin saying "no." Outside events beyond our control influence our time management. To avoid losing your mind over the unexpected, have a plan #2, #3, and so on, in mind. Good planning allows for flexibility. Who we are influences our time management. As a professional, make sure that poor planning, poor personal organization, or procrastination do not eat up your time. Allow room in your plans for your character!

Our goals should be the major influence on our time management. Have you written down your life-time goals? Ten year goals? Yearly and weekly goals? Having these goals listed helps to evaluate your progress. Planning is essential if you want to accomplish your life-time goals instead of having your life frittered away on inconsequential events. Try the Swiss cheese philosophy Alan Lakein advocates. This involves nibbling away at a big project in little chunks, until the whole project is completed. You may have to nibble the whole way to your big goals, but steady nibbling (remember the tortoise and the hare) will get you there.

Be alert to time management practices. Reading about them is inspirational. Begin by reading the two articles included in this manual. They will tell you how other home economists have met their time demands.

THE 15 GOLDEN RULES FOR SUCCESS AS A MANAGER

by
Flora L. Williams
Assistant Professor
Department of Home Management
and Family Economics
School of Home Economics
Purdue University
West Lafayette, Indiana

As a home economist, you often have more to do than you think you can do in the time available.

But if you rearrange your ideas about managing time and resources, could you not accomplish more than you do now? If you apply correct management concepts to your work, you could reap dividends in additional time for other projects and in added satisfaction in your work.

Successful management is the organizer that lets you get the most value from the resources you have at your disposal. By mastering your ability to manage human relations, your work, and your leisure, you will achieve the power to develop your human potential to its greatest extent.

Good managers share a number of positive qualities that have made them successful. These qualities are, in effect, rules for success in management, because without following many of them, a manager cannot be effective. If you are a good manager, then, you have many of the following characteristics:

1. **You are a realist.**
- You keep things in perspective by focusing on objectives that fit into your framework of both long-term and short-term goals. You are aware that everyday activities can forward your future plans, but you are careful that such short-term activities do not work counter to your long-term goals or your ultimate values.

   You are also aware that every piece of your experience fits into the long-term picture. For example, as a student interested in a career in restaurant management, you accept a job in a restaurant waiting on tables to earn money for your education and to teach you something at first-hand about restaurants, but you turn down another job selling children's toys in a store because it has no relation to your long-term goal.

- You are not a "tightrope walker," but are adept at—and realistic about—the fine art of balancing demands on your time. You recognize that the only workable schedule is a flexible one allowing time for family, friends, professional activities, hobbies, special interests, and an adequate amount of rest.

J. Home Economics / September 1974, permission granted.

- As a realist, you design and carry out plans to achieve your goals. You have drive; you are on the move, and you live in an exciting environment. You have a sense of urgency about achieving goals.
- From a number of desirable and interesting goals, you have chosen some you consider most worthwhile and have ranked them in order of priority. (You have observed that those who are unable to rank their goals become nearly neurotic with the effort of reconciling the strains created by the pull of equal goals.)

2. You are self-reliant, self-contained, and self-starting.
- You know when to lead and when to take the initiative. You make things happen. You reject the role of passive observer who complains about the turn events have taken without ever having done anything to make those events turn out differently.
- You do not spend much time worrying about the "image of home economists." Instead, you make your unique professional contribution to the life of your community by being able to relate— and to communicate—the implications of government policies on families. You demonstrate the value of home economics by your creative use of scarce resources and by your use of successful management techniques.
- By carrying out your professional responsibilities, you create respect in the community for yourself and for your role as a home economist. Your judgment is accepted by the community.

3. You are creative.
- You are often the one to "do something different." You push yourself to think of alternative possibilities when doing tasks. You analyze new ideas and develop new techniques. You foresee opportunities.
- You have the creative ability to look at activities and programs from the perspective of the family and suggest changes, add or eliminate components, obtain more value for the money spent or the energy expended, and imagine events in the future that may relate to the benefits or problems being considered.

4. You are a creature of habit.
- Your ability to develop useful routines has reduced the need for continual decision making and has greatly enhanced the quality of your life by giving you a more secure and stable environment.
- After you have evaluated new methods or products, you have standardized their uses so that you can concentrate your energy on exploring other developments and on the creative and the unusual.

5. You are flexible.
- Because you perform at different levels of efficiency at different times in the day, you have learned to adapt your daily schedule to allow for efficiency peaks and lows.
- You change plans or program or products when you have added knowledge or different needs.
- You change plans, programs, or products when you have added You are not chained to one approach to problems, to one life-style, or to particular methods. As the needs of your profession and of

society change, you are able to adapt your career plans to these changes, developing the skills and services that are most in demand.

6. You have varying standards of perfection.

- You make adjustments if you cannot meet the standards you desire. You do this by: a) changing or lowering your standards, b) becoming more efficient, or c) increasing your resources.
- You are able to "let go" of unimportant details.

7. You work hard and efficiently.

- You have positive attitudes about work. You have the necessary professional skills to do your work well, you have the health and energy needed to work at a sustained pace over long periods of time, you are *willing* to work and to take responsibility, and you have the ambition and the enthusiasm to carry out your work plans.
- As a professional and as a supervisor of others, you are aware that it takes more than knowledge or creative ideas to implement plans—it takes hard work, and it is the hard worker who is successful.
- Even though you work hard, you do not use more energy, time, equipment, or emotions than are needed to get the job done at the necessary standard. You continuously apply the principles of time and motion economy: you eliminate unnecessary tasks or elements, you simplify or combine others, or you consider whether to rearrange the space or sequence between them. You have learned that regret, fear, conflict, and worry waste inner resources and make work more difficult.
- You continually strive to increase both the quantity and quality of your work output, and to decrease tension and your input of resources in whatever you do.

8. You learn from experience—from your own and from that of others.

- You have learned that *any* experience—including those that have been unhappy or unpleasant for you—can be a learning situation if you see the experience that way and use it for reevaluation and reassessment.
- You learn from your mistakes. They keep you humble, sincere, and striving. Your mistakes teach you both what *not* to do in the future and how to be more understanding of others.

9. You stay alert by continuously seeking new knowledge.

- When you have acquired new knowledge, you "process" it, sometimes for storage and later retrieval and use, sometimes for immediate use. Your ability to process information gives you the vital tools you need for efficient management because you have found that decisions are difficult when knowledge is inadequate.
- Because you have learned that there is often a gap in time between acquiring knowledge and its later use, you have learned a variety of devices to help you process this information: to organize information conceptually in mental drawers or compartments, to keep notes on paper, to keep files.

10. You enjoy making decisions and taking responsibility.

- Your conscious attitude is that you *can* change a situation that needs changing. You have learned to remove yourself sufficiently from the problem, to identify it, to see possible reasons why it has occurred, to consider alternatives, and to outline the steps to be followed to solve the problem and produce change for the better.

- You are optimistic about the change implied in decision making because you recognize that there are choices. You are aware that, while some problems do work themselves out over time, there are other problems that become intensified if not faced.

11. You are willing to take risks.

- Your ability to take risks comes from self-confidence, faith, material security, and past experience. Past failures of your own or of others have not killed your willingness to try new things or stifled your hope of success. You are not chained to one approach to problems, to one life-style, or to a rigid list of products you find acceptable.

- You have the courage to approach even those who seem unapproachable. When you are scared, you remind yourself that you have lived through previous difficult or terrifying experiences and come out of them all the better for having done so.

12. You know when to act and seize opportunity when it knocks and when to wait for more information.

- You can move quickly to make use of an opportunity before it is lost forever, but before doing so, you have learned to check both your list of wants and your own information-processing and retrieval system to ensure that you have sufficient information to act wisely.

13. You have the ability to communicate easily and clearly with others.

- In managing others, you initiate communication and check on clarity of understanding. You have artful ways of seeing that your meaning is clearly understood—you might ask others to explain a principle, to describe how they are going to accomplish certain tasks, or to relate what they have heard to other factors.

- You are able to make yourself clearly understood. When it is necessary to do so, you can clarify the statements of others so that general communication within a group is possible.

- When others speak, you show that you are willing to understand them by listening carefully to both their verbal and their nonverbal messages to you.

14. You are able to follow others as well as to lead them.

- You have long been aware that there are many different ways of performing these tasks if they are satisfying basic work objectives.

- You develop leadership in others by giving them these opportunities to express themselves. You allow others the freedom to make mistakes, so that through experience, they will learn to develop confidence, skill, and wisdom.

- As a successful manager, you have learned to gain the cooperation of those who will carry out your work-related goals. You have their cooperation because you have involved them in the setting of those goals.

15. You are able to bring out the best in others by helping them to develop their inner resources.

- In managing a group, you divide responsibility according to the economic principle of comparative advantage—that is, you encourage the least able persons to do the tasks they do best and the most able persons to do the tasks that only they can do—so that each member of the group feels challenged and none feels overworked or resentful.

In summary, then, you as a skillful manager know when to change environments and when to adjust to them. You are determined enough to do what you have planned, but wise enough to change your plans at times. You hold to standards, but adjust as the need arises.

As a wise manager, you sometimes bend to the needs of others. You hold tight to what is right but bend in order not to break. You find that your purpose in living is achieved by serving others. You develop inner strength by building resources with firm foundations, by reaching to the heavens, and by yielding to the currents of the times when wisdom dictates.

YOUR IMAGE IS SHOWING

Image, image, image. AHEA spent extensive dollars to determine the image of our profession. Corporate executives spend anywhere from $40,000 for image analysis to $25 for a shopping trip. Books like John Molloy's *Dress for Success* end up on the best seller list. As a beginning professional, can you afford to ignore this business of image?

True, image does not replace qualifications. Image does give you the opportunity to prove your qualifications. Reread the quotation preceding this discussion. You have probably caught on already to the fact that attractive people usually have more options open to them. Or, as Richard Bolles put it in *Go Hire Yourself an Employer,* "A good first appearance gets you a free pass to first base." Attractiveness and unattractiveness are not immutable qualities but depend most upon your attention to dress, grooming and personal appearance.

Your image is important even after the interview and after you have the job. The transition from being a student to being a professional has its own special problems. Don't let a student image undermine your competence as a professional. Look like you are qualified to do the job.

We recognize a doctor by a stethoscope, a postman by a blue uniform, and an executive by an expensively tailored suit and briefcase. Most professional home economists don't have such badges to wear. Still, if you think, you can probably conjure up a vision of a professional home economist..

. . . YOUR IMAGE

There are several routes you can take to develop your own professional look. Immerse yourself in reading the numerous articles and some of the books that deal with dressing for the job. Reading will give you a general idea of how some professionals think professionals should dress, what is acceptable in different parts of the country, how to assemble a "professional" wardrobe, and reasons for a particular style of dress. Although most of what has been written is geared for corporate executives and business, many of the principles are useful for home economics in other areas. What has been written is by no means law, but reading will create an awareness of the importance of professional appearance and will give you ideas about how to achieve your own.

Look at periodicals geared toward your profession. What are the people wearing in the pictures? Who advertises clothing and what do their lines look like?

What is in the stores? Look at the career departments in the better stores for ideas. Browsing will give you a feel for what quality, styles and lines the professionals in your city buy.

Adopting a model can be a big help to a graduate just starting out in the work world. The model can be someone you work with or better yet, according to Molloy, someone who holds the position you are working toward. What do they look like? What do they wear? How can you achieve the same competent image and still be you? Sometimes seeing a model is the quickest and easiest way to get an overall picture effect of grooming and dress that is appropriate for the job.

What you wear will speak louder than what you say. It is to your advantage to make sure your clothing communicates the non-verbal message your employer wants to hear. Clothing communicates attitudes. Studies have shown that people are more influenced by other people who are dressed like themselves. This is partly because if someone looks like you, you can't help but assume that they think like you. If you want to present an authoritative appearance, dress the part. Authoritative dressing is usually dressing a couple of notches above the person "under" you. Dressing "up" implies making sure that what you are wearing is quality, in impeccable condition, coordinated and looks good on you. You feel confident in this kind of outfit. As Voltaire observed, "dress changes the manners." Graduates just beginning in the work world need this extra boost to overcome the "inexperienced and therefore, not-as-competent" prejudice that clients and employers and colleagues are prone to have. Young teachers need to dress more authoritatively than older ones. Young professionals trying to get an idea across to more experienced professionals or clients will benefit by looking competent. Dressing authoritatively is not always the answer. Reporters have found that if they look "better" and of a higher status than someone from whom they are trying to get information, their source may distrust them. You may be expected to dress more flamboyantly in fields like fashion merchandising or public relations. You must decide where you fit between dressing up and dressing down for your job effectiveness. A person who ignores the unwritten guidelines for appearance may be jeopardizing a career. Someone has said, "I prefer to work within the system because I prefer to eat."

. . . IN TERMS OF DOLLARS AND CENTS

Making the transition between the college look and the professional look doesn't always have to be expensive. If you are short on the resource of money, you can compensate by using your brain to plan and your time to shop. As always, planning begins with assessment. What do you have and what do you need? The "Career Wardrobe Planning Outline" included in this chapter may help you begin planning.

Some hints to aid in planning:
1. Separates can be more versatile than one-piece outfits.
2. Neutral colors are less memorable than other colors so you can get away with more repeats by changing accessories, shirts, blouses, etc.
3. Classic, rather than faddish styles, tend to be more versatile and do not need to be replaced year after year. If you feel it is appropriate for your job, and you want to wear more faddish clothes, try combining a touch of fad in accessories with your classic separates.
4. In this country, conservative dressing *implies* character qualities that employers value; stability, maturity and honesty are examples. You may wish to consider this when choosing your professional wardrobe.

When funds run short . . .

Imagination must take over when wealth hasn't. A general rule of thumb or probability is that if you shop often enough, you'll probably come across a good deal. Here are some suggestions:

- If at all possible, write out your wardrobe plan and begin filling in the gaps a year in advance. Set aside money to take advantage of seasonal sales promotions and that occasional "find." Classic lines or more conservative dress do not age year after year and sales are a good way to begin your collection.

- Molloy has developed a technique of "cross-sectional shopping." Briefly this involves: determining what you need to buy. Write down about three alternatives. For instance, you need something to wear to work. A blue suit, gray suit or tan suit would work. With this in mind, go to the most expensive store in town and look at your top three choices. Notice *detail,* the exact color, texture of the fabric, buttons, style and cut, and accessories displayed with it. Next, go to the least expensive store in town and try to match the three choices. What ensemble comes the closest in matching color, texture, fabric, buttons, style and cut? Now, go to the expensive store again and look carefully at the choices that were not eliminated at the cheaper store. Finally, go to a store that sells within your price range. Which of your choices is duplicated there? Choose the most expensive looking one that matches the choice in the expensive store.

- There are outlet stores available in some areas of the country. Sometimes you can buy famous-name clothes in little rooms adjoining manufacturing plants. If some of these clothes are "seconds" you may be able to make the necessary repairs and walk away well-dressed and still be in the black.

- If you are lucky, you can stake out an ensemble in an expensive store and follow it through its series of markdowns. It takes a lot of nerve and patience to follow something you want all the way to the budget basement, but it can pay. These cycles usually last the entire season. The season may change before you see the final markdown that makes it a real possibility for you.

- Buy some clothes at an inexpensive or discount store and then change the trim or buttons. Many times, buttons can make the difference in price between outfits.

- Do you have a strong hunter's instinct? Adventurous shoppers may find usable clothes at garage sales, second-hand stores or flea markets. People sell perfectly good clothes because they have outgrown them, they never fit in the first place, the color was all wrong, or some other reason. Your own closet probably has some of these items. If you are talented at sewing, you are even more likely to find something you can use with a bit of alteration.

- In the beginning of your career, you may choose to skimp on clothing and buy expensive accessories. After all, how many people wear $45 shoes with a $10 suit? It is easier to recognize quality in accessories. No one may ever suspect your cleverness.

- If you are able to sew well, or know someone who can sew for you, you may be able to save money. You may choose to make a simple skirt from good material and then buy a jacket. Close attention to fit and current styles and fabrics can make you look custom-made rather than homemade. It would be false economy if the finished look fell short of the professional image desired.

- You and a same-sized friend could pool your resources until you are able to assemble a complete wardrobe. Needless to say, some guidelines would have to be set up, but sharing can cut expenses.

. . . YOUR IDEAS

_____

_____

_____

_____

_____

_____

_____

_____

_____

_____

_____

_____

_____

_____

_____

_____

_____

_____

. . . LOOSE ENDS

Women, especially, must be conscious of how their bodies look in their clothes. Looking suggestively sexy is out of place in a professional position. As one woman professional in Cleveland says, "You have to tread a narrow line between looking like a castrating female and looking open to any proposition. Because once you have to discuss whether or not you'll go to bed—you're out of work." Many women have found that crisp, classic suits, dresses, and blazers and skirts get the reaction they wish from their colleagues. Femininely tailored seems to be the consensus in the literature.

Anything you choose to wear is going to look better on a trim body in good shape. Firmness, rather than softness, implies a sense of energy and efficiency on the job. Employers tend to discriminate against applicants who are overweight. Since weight is something under *your* control, it would be a shame to let it influence your effectiveness.

Anything you choose to wear will look better if you are well-groomed. Again, look at the people who are now where you want to be in your profession. What seem to be the most acceptable hairstyles?

For men, are beards, moustaches, and sideburns acceptable? Both men and women professionals will benefit from good haircuts that are easily maintained. Shop and ask around for a good stylist. Clean, healthy hair preserves any professional look.

If you have paid careful attention to dress and hairstyle and something still does not look quite right, you may want to try different makeup. Salespersons close in age, whose makeup seems appropriate and who sell more than one line, can be a valuable resource in getting just the right look.

Poor hygiene and careless grooming can kill any look. Garlic breath, body odor, oily or limp hair or broken, rough nails will not contribute anything positive to your image. Dress details like runny nylons, worn heels, scuffed shoes, missing buttons, or soiled clothing will destroy the look you are trying to achieve.

. . . FROM INSIDE OUT

Health practice invariably shows up in your appearance and performance. In the hectic pace of professional life, even you can suffer from nutritional deficiencies that zap energy and that can leave you irritable. It takes determination to pass up a rich carbohydrate and grab something with more nutrients when you are in a hurry. Many people experience a midmorning slump around 10:00. This is caused by a drop in blood sugar. Contrary to what you might think, a candy bar accentuates the problem. Instead, you need a protein food. Keep something like cheese and crackers on hand instead of doughnuts. "Post-prandial" droop is another energy zapper. This is the term for that uncontrollable urge to sleep after a meal. Not everyone experiences this. If you do, try to plan your day to take this into consideration. It may help to change your lunchtime menu.

Exercise is therapeutic. You have probably been relatively motionless from 8:00 to 5:00 every day. Your brain is far more tired than your body. Some fast exercise or a brisk walk to your car parked a mile away can help you think more efficiently. Regular, vigorous exercise (if your health permits) enhances sleep at night, too. Kenneth Cooper's *Aerobics* plan is a very inspirational one for the benefits of exercise. Professionals all over the country have caught on to the benefits of tension release through exercise.

An effective form of oriental torture was to allow a prisoner to fall asleep for one hour and then to wake him. He was never allowed to sleep more than one hour at a time. This ancient form of torture surfaces today and most of the time is self-inflicted. Sleep is the commodity often cut short when time runs short. Losing a few nights here and there will not wreak permanent damage to your system, but a continual lack of sleep will cost you in efficiency and foolish mental errors. You have to decide how much sleep your body needs. Most people need from 6½ to 8½ hours per night. Sleep deprivation can indirectly lead to food deprivation if it causes you to be a bumbling employee.

Ignoring the unwritten codes for appearance as a professional can cost you in ways you do not even realize. It takes too much energy to convince someone of your competence if your manner of dress contradicts your effectiveness. Remember the quote from Richard Bolles about appearance: "A good first appearance gets you a free pass to first base . . ."? He finished the statement with, "and that's all. From then on, you have to circle the bases with talent." Clothing does not replace skills but it can be used to convey competence and your sense of purpose. You'll know you have achieved the look when you feel confident enough to forget about what you are wearing and how you look and to get on with your business!

WORK SHEET
CAREER WARDROBE PLANNING OUTLINE

1) List three ideas that you want your clothing to communicate to others in your anticipated world of work.

a)

b)

c)

2) Will your present wardrobe communicate these ideas?

___ YES   ___ NO

3) What percentage of your wardrobe is wearable? ___ %

4) What percentage could easily be made wearable? ___ %

5) Will your wardrobe need major changes for your new career?

___ YES   ___ NO

If you checked YES, let's do a little paper work to see what clothing you have that can be used. You may just be surprised what you can make into workable outfits.

WEARABLE CLOTHING

SUITS	COATS/BLAZERS
TROUSERS/SKIRTS	SHIRTS/BLOUSES
VESTS	DRESSES

ACCESSORIES

WORKABLE OUTFITS FROM WEARABLE CLOTHING

1)	2)
3)	4)
5)	6)

WORKABLE OUTFITS WITH ADDITION OF ONE NEW ITEM

The new item goes on the line, the rest of the outfit below the new item. Remember that this new item should be used for making at least three new outfits.

1)_____	2)_____
1a)	2a)
1b)	2b)
3)_____	4)_____
3a)	4a)
3b)	

Prepared in consultation with Patricia Taylor Griffin, 1978 graduate.

Dressing for
the Office

Women have come a long way, baby, and all that.
More are trying to go higher in the business hierarchy than ever before.
How should an ambitious female executive dress?
Does she emulate men?
Keep her feminity?
Carry both a briefcase and a handbag?

By Diane Duston

In her five-by-eight cubicle with walls that don't quite reach the ceiling, Barbara Arwood, a consultant for the Ohio Department of Education writes reports, organizes meetings, and helps push around the papers that keep government in action. She is serious about her job and her desire to move into business management. She dresses tastefully, perhaps with more flair than the average middle-level bureaucrat, but with a great deal of thought about the effect her clothes will have on her job. She feels she must dress in a way that is acceptable to those she works for: few people know that if she could, she'd strut into her office in satin, sequins, and bangles.

If you look closely, you'll see hints to the flamboyant side of her personality. There's that feather she wears around her neck, and the silver "E" on a chain that she bought because she liked its shape better than "B" or her other initials. But she'll never wear her glittery, silver four-inch platform shoes to the office. They're tucked away at home with her feather boa.

Arwood used to dress any crazy way she felt, but now at 30, she wants to put her master's degree to work. "It takes too much energy to get people to listen to you if you are dressed funny," she says. During a dinner break from shopping one evening, she leaned across the table and said earnestly, "Look, you could have the secret to life, but if you're dressed too far-out, no one will even listen to you."

Surely, by now anyone interested in wearing the clothes that will do the most for his or her career has heard of John T. Molloy and his books on dressing for success. For women, he advocates a conservative, skirted two-piece suit in a dark color and good fabric, worn with modest blouse and plain shoes. It's a dull combination. But businesswomen have to decide for themselves whether that look is the appropriate one for them and for their offices.

Even after you've selected the outfit you feel perfectly fits the image you are after, how do you know whether the person shaking your hand for the first time or the one handing out promotions is getting the right picture? It's obvious from the myriad clothing combinations sold and worn that individual taste knows no bounds.

Besides, can a 5-foot, 2-inch, 100-pound 30-year-old who looks the same as she did the day she graduated from high school be transformed into an authority figure with a change of wardrobe? Will the woman with the figure of Miss Universe who also holds an MBA and a law degree kill her chances at upper level management by wearing V-necks? If you have Barbara Arwood's creative flair, how far can you go and still fit into state government work, for example?

Traditionally it has been acceptable for women to spend a great deal of time and energy poring over fashion magazines, attending style shows, taking long shopping trips, consulting designers, dressing themselves and looking into the mirror. And possibly that *modus operandi* may still be the norm; but today a woman may be dressing not to turn men on sexually, but to try to impress them with legal, mathematical, journalistic, engineering, architectural or managerial skills. Perhaps it can't be done, but most believe the clothes you wear make such a strong impression on others that it's not worth taking the chance.

All the women we talked to emphatically agreed that clothes affect a woman's upward mobility in her profession.

Nancy Lawson is absolutely sure of it. Lawson is a woman with credentials; among other things she was valedictorian of her law school class. She practiced public service law for awhile in a government-funded firm and then, still thousands of dollars in debt from educational loans, went on a shopping spree to improve her wardrobe. Viewing the effort as an investment, she bought nothing but the finest. A few months later, while questioning a prominent attorney in another city on research he had done in an area of law she was pursuing for a case, Lawson was offered a job. Now an associate in the attorney's firm, she credits the job offer partly to the fact that she was well-dressed during the interview.

"An attorney should look successful," Lawson says. "And you should not look dowdy. No one wants to have someone around who looks frumpy."

Lawson still dishes out the big bucks for clothes. "You have to set yourself off from the secretaries," she says. "Men in an office are presumed to be in authority, but women are presumed to be secretaries."

Elizabeth De Villing, an attorney and director of advanced underwriting for the Midland Mutual Life Insurance Co., tells of an experience she had in the elevator of her multi-story office building. The building houses several law firms as well as the insurance company, and there are many female employees, mostly at the clerical level. "Two women riding in the elevator said to me one day, 'We've been watching you for several months. You're an attorney, aren't you? We can tell by the way you dress.' I thought that was a nice compliment," she says.

"It's mandatory that a woman in business dress professionally," says Zoe McCathrin, assistant vice president for BancOhio Corp. Her assistant, Pam Church, says a woman should dress the way she wants to be treated. She says she spends 25 to 30 per cent of her salary on clothes because she feels quality is important in achieving the look that fits her ambitions. "Every woman should have at least one good suit for each season," Church says.

McCathrin says she passes up many casual outfits she would like to buy because they don't fit the banking image. The banking industry is conservative, she says; "It's been a tough road for women in banking. We don't need to do anything that would hurt our credibility."

During the 1960s, hard-core feminists, particularly those on college campuses, believed preoccupation with clothes was a frivolity that detracted from woman as man's equal. To co-eds of those days, fatigue jackets and blue jeans were the uniform and many graduated with great disdain for fashion-consciousness. Gloria Steinem once shocked the women's movement by wearing a backless blouse and miniskirt to a feminist gathering.

WHAT THE BOSSES SAY

William J. Brown, attorney general, State of Ohio—"When I'm judging a woman lawyer I'm interested mainly in the basic qualifications. But it just seems to me that the lawyers who move upward also dress well. Maryann Gall, who used to be chief legal counsel—the first woman chief counsel in the attorney general's office—always looked nice. She almost always wore a suit. We have a dress code for everyone in the office. No denim. I don't want any girl walking around here in a goddamned halter top and a pair of blue jeans."

Ron Cowman, president, Kight, Cowman, Abram Inc.—"I'm a bad judge of what would be the best outfit for a woman in an executive position. There is no uniform. A woman has to have good taste. She can usually tell for herself. If we think someone has talent and capability and hasn't recognized the importance of clothes, we'll talk to them about it."

Robert Duncan, judge, U.S. District Court—"I don't have any objections to pantsuits on women. The cut of the thing is important, not too frilly. Dress should conform to the formal atmosphere of the court. By and large, attorneys understand the psychology of the court. It's a business of persuasion. Oh, occasionally you'll see a lawyer in a bit of a race-track outfit. Some can get away with it. People should dress to fit their personalities. I would not be affected by the way a lawyer was dressed in judging the argument, but a jury might be. I would imagine that initial perceptions of the jurors would be made on the way attorneys are dressed."

George E. Tyack, judge, Franklin County Common Pleas Court—"I never gave it much thought, but there is no doubt in my mind that a woman lawyer should dress in a businesslike manner. I don't object to nice pantsuits. Traditionally the courtroom is very conservative, but now sport coats are very common on the men, even in corduroy."

Robert G. Stevens, president and chairman of the board, BancOhio Corp.—"If you are in an organization and want people to perceive you as a person of responsibility you have to look around and see how people who have achieved that responsibility look. It's like being in a play. If you play doctor, it helps the audience to recognize your role if you have a stethoscope around your neck. People are in a hurry to develop perceptions. It helps if you look the part you represent. In some ways a woman has a more difficult time because there are not the well-defined stereotypes for women executives. You see successful women emulating men with vests and jackets. People get promoted when they start acting the new role. Clothes help."

Rick Townley, news director, Channel 4—"Clothing reflects professionalism, credibility. If someone goes on the air with a particularly gaudy outfit, the viewers will focus on that instead of what is being said. One of the ways women newscasters go about giving a credible impression is to show that this is not show business and that they are journalists, not fashion models. I've seen some women on the networks with low-cut necklines and it sort of bothered me. Whatever is worn should not attract more attention than what the woman is saying."

Franklin B. Walter, Ohio superintendent of public instruction—"Male or female should project a neat appearance. A woman can be appropriately dressed in an attractive pantsuit or dress. The way a person moves and the posture is indicative of energy and determination to succeed in a job."

Ralph Waldo, president, Columbus Mutual Life Insurance Co.—"I would like to have my employees dress so that if they are called into my office they'll feel comfortable. A person who is well-dressed usually is a good worker. I don't particularly like pants on women, but I can understand how in cold weather they prefer them. Dress codes are extremely hard to enforce."

Waldo referred to a problem with a woman employee who came to work in a rather scant halter top one hot summer day. She caused some commotion as men from other parts of the building all suddenly seemed to have business in the office in which she was working. "She was told to go home and change," Waldo says. "I couldn't find any of my company officers."

—D.D.

Times have changed since then. Today's women still want to be taken seriously by their male peers, but they don't think they need to look purposely plain or masculine to prove equality. "Women who appear masculine interest me," McCathrin says. "I don't understand them. I think they think it is a part of being accepted. But they can go too far."

"It's a mistake to appear too masculine," Nora Moushey, an actuary for Columbus Mutual Life Insurance Co., says. "After all, you are a woman."

But if appearing too masculine is a mistake, appearing too sexy is a bigger one, women agree. Too much exposed bosom or leg are sure detriments to business success, they say.

In the movie *Network,* Faye Dunaway played an aggressive, ambitious television vice president who commanded respect from all who dared cross her path. Dunaway played a character who was ruthless, selfish and success-oriented—a refreshing change from the majority of past Hollywood portrayals. But the point here is that while Faye wore beautiful clothes which were mostly tailored, one thing she didn't wear was a bra. It didn't seem to impede *her* upward mobility, but have you ever known a woman executive who didn't wear a bra? Bralessness used to be a symbol of sorts of women's liberation, but were those braless women ever taken seriously in the business world? Do visible nipples a la the Farrah Fawcett poster have a place in the boardroom?

"You can't dress in a way that would distract from your work," Moushey says. "I sometimes don't wear a bra at home, but I'd never go without one at work. And I wouldn't wear a skirt too short. If you dress in short, sexy clothes, people will remember you as the girl who wore the sexy dress to work, not as the woman who presented a good report."

Jodi Hawk, second vice president and director of personnel at Columbus Mutual, is the kind of woman who easily draws whistles from admiring males. She loves good clothes and spends a lot of money on them. But she warns against a sexy image and chooses a tailored look for herself.

"I've been in my job long enough that I can get away with a lot more freedom in what I wear," she says. "I always try to look nice, but it makes me mad when men react to me sexually in a business situation."

Elizabeth De Villing also admits encountering wolfish comments from men she meets in the insurance business. She's youthful looking and attractive. Do her looks ever keep her from being taken seriously by men? "Yes," she says, "Until I open my mouth. I travel a lot in my business and I've never had a business associate make a pass at me. I dress to be respected. I try to keep up with the latest styles, but I would consider myself a conservative dresser. I don't want to look faddy or sexy. I've always enjoyed clothes and looking nice. I've got a lot more clothes than I ever wear.

"It's said in this business that since we deal in big dollars, it is important to look as if you are used to big dollars. I think a nice-looking woman has a real advantage in business, but she won't get far if she doesn't know what she's doing," De Villing says.

Most women mention some clothes they would like to buy but don't because they don't fit the image they are trying to project. Moushey mentioned a jersey jumpsuit she liked but felt was inappropriate for the office. Margaret Ann Samuels, an assistant Ohio attorney general, says she'd dress in more of a peasant look if she could. Susan Scheutzow, a state senator's legislative assistant, says she passes up many things she considers too pretty or too soft-looking.

A word used repeatedly in connection with dressing for work was "appropriate." But even though the word kept creeping into conversation, its meaning differed with the job the woman had or the company for which she worked.

"I'd almost have to come in here naked to be criticized for my appearance," Patty Russell, media director for the advertising firm of Kight, Cowman, Abram Inc. says. "Oh, wait a minute, I do have one outfit my boss doesn't like. I was in the Marine Corps and so was he. I have a pants outfit that is a sailor suit. He says I'm being a traitor when I wear it.

"In an advertising agency you can get away with a more casual look," Russell says. "You can't come in to work in a shirt and jeans any more than a guy could. I do feel that how you dress affects your job. I usually wear pantsuits, sometimes a skirt. Not platform shoes or high heels. When I go out of the office I always wear a nice pantsuit. But I'm usually lugging materials around so I have to dress in a way that is practical for that."

Another woman in the same company has a slightly different attitude about her clothes.

Linda Harrison, vice president of business development, came up through the ranks and her wardrobe changed along the way. In seven years she went from a secretary who sometimes wore blue jeans to a vice president who now prefers skirted three-piece suits.

"I'm a firm believer that clothes are important in the job," Harrison says. "I think performance is the key but I think clothes help. When I started here I was wearing mini-skirts and pants. I looked like a college girl. When I started handling accounts I was told to change the way I dressed. At that time I needed to be told because I was rebellious and believed that people should accept me for what I was, not how I looked."

Harrison is 26 and says that since she is younger than most of her clients it is especially important to her to dress professionally. "But it's a bitch in this city to find the proper clothes," she says. "The stores are just not geared to the professional woman. I'd like to go on a shopping spree in Chicago or someplace where they are used to career women."

Harrison's job is to develop business for her firm. She says it is important to dress stylishly because it says something about the company. "We are advertising people and we want to present an innovative, forward-looking impression."

Another woman whose wardrobe changed with her job is Estelle Lehring. Now in public relations for Warner QUBE, Lehring once worked in public relations for Ohio State University Hospitals. "At OSU I definitely did not dress the way I'm dressing now. I was not as together. But I didn't have the contact with the outside world. I spent a lot of the time at my desk.

"Now I think I'm more mature about it. I've noticed that those women who are successful are paying attention to what they wear. You have to look the part."

Lehring says she dresses according to whom she is going to see. She classifies her clothes as tailored but not "super conservative." "My skirts are below the knee. I wear slacks and sweaters. I wear lots of jewelry. A minimum of four rings, bracelets, thin gold necklaces."

Success in some professions depends as much on the general public's perceptions as those of the boss.

Vicki Grant, news reporter and noon anchorperson on Channel 4, must present the image of a woman who knows what she is talking about to the thousands of Columbus area residents who depend upon her for information about their city. She finds some are paying an incredible amount of attention to how she looks. Suggestions from viewers on clothing are not uncommon.

"People tell me, 'That color is not right for you,' or, 'That color looks good on you,' People sometimes get tired of seeing scarves and say I shouldn't wear so many scarves."

She tells of a letter from a viewer criticizing her for wearing something that was "too low cut." "I had a hard time figuring out what dress they were talking about," she says. Grant has one dress that no one else thought was low cut, though it dipped slightly below her neck. "I won't try to guess what the age of the person who wrote was, but it must have been someone who expects to see only turtlenecks."

Grant says she can't recall the men who appear on camera getting the kind of criticism she and the other women receive. "But it doesn't bother me," she says. "Most of it is constructive. You develop a thick skin in this business."

Grant's colleague, Michelle Gailiun, is remembered by many newsmakers and reporters for the transition in her appearance when she moved from behind the camera to in front of it. She dresses stylishly in tailored clothing now, but a matter of months ago, as a camerawoman for Electro-Media, Inc., she tromped around the Statehouse in blue jeans and sturdy shoes, often with a knitted stocking cap pulled down over her hair.

"Everyone has remarked on the change," Gailiun says. "Even Woody Hayes."

"Back then I had to do a lot of camera work and had to dress more practically. I never used to think about what I wore until I started being on TV. I really don't feel comfortable talking about this. Basically, I feel a person should dress so that viewers don't notice what you have on. Gen-earally, I buy what I like. But I don't buy anything with frilly cuffs. And low necklines are taboo. I didn't go on a shopping spree or anything when I took this job. I had a lot of clothes that I hadn't worn for a long time. I bought conservative things that hold up. I'm still wearing a skirt that I had my freshman year at Sweet Briar."

Gailiun says newsmakers react to her a little differently now than when she was doing camera work, but she feels it has more to do with the change in her job function than in her wardrobe. "Though I did have one person say to me, 'You cleaned up pretty good,' " she laughs.

Most women agree that success depends in large part on being noticed by those in power. Clothing can be an asset to visibility. Be tailored, not dowdy; stylish, not faddish; attractive, not sexy, women say.

In some jobs clothes are not as important as in others. When questioned about how she feels about clothes in her profession, Diane Reichwein, a Franklin County social worker, said, "I'm not really a good person to ask. I've always tried to think about what I wear in relation to my job. But you should see what they wear around here. Until they instituted a dress code you couldn't tell the workers from the recipients. And you know what the dress code was? Things like 'no blue jeans, no t-shirts, no bedroom slippers.' "

*Diane Duston is a wire service
reporter in Columbus.*

THE EXECUTIVE ACCESSORIES

The woman on the rise should be aware of three basic accoutrements no business executive worth his or her picture window view of the city would be without.

First is the Cross pen. That's the brand name for a gold or silver pen that comes with matching mechanical pencil. Assistant bank vice president Zoe McCathrin says she didn't know how important the Cross pen was until she went to her first board meeting. "All the men pulled out their Cross pens," she says. "I was glad I had one, too." The sign of the person who has really made it is a Cross pen desk set, she adds.

Second is the appointment book, preferably with name or monogram embossed on the cover. It is essential to have this in an easily obtainable place for quick reference. Men usually carry them in an inside suit coat pocket. Women should keep theirs in a purse pocket or other convenient spot. Digging through a cluttered handbag or dumping contents of same onto a boardroom table in search of the appointment book kills the effect.

Last, but certainly not least, is the briefcase. This is the most interesting of all business accessories because it is so obvious and of such great variety.

A woman with a briefcase is never mistaken for a file clerk, but she is in a slightly different situation than the man. Because she usually also carries a purse, the woman with a briefcase has two pieces of baggage to lug around. Everything carried in a handbag probably could be tucked into a briefcase, but purses have become such a habit, things of security, occupation for the hands. They are difficult to dispense with.

"I carry both a purse and a briefcase and I think it's a big pain in the neck," insurance actuary Nora Moushey says. "I think it's disgraceful that women's clothes don't have more pockets. I would like to not carry a purse, but I've never found a piece of equipage that could serve as both." Moushey says she also would like to see briefcases in nicer colors for women.

McCathrin pulled out a white, distinctly feminine briefcase from behind her desk to illustrate her preference. "My husband got me a briefcase when I got my first promotion. I wanted white because I didn't want it to look like a man's . . . it was a way of thumbing my nose at the men." McCathrin's complaint is that briefcases are too heavy.

Okay. So you're a woman executive walking to a business meeting with your male associates. You're about 5-foot-4 and slightly built and you're laboring under the weight of an oversized handbag and a briefcase. Do you let one of the men carry your briefcase for you if he asks? One woman attorney says her male associate is always trying to carry her briefcase and she finds it embarrassing. "Can you imagine someone else carrying *your* briefcase?" she asks in astonishment.

Perhaps the answer is to avoid looking overburdened by keeping the size of your purse to a minimum or using a clutch bag that can be placed inside the briefcase.

Despite the problems facing the woman with a briefcase, there are advantages, too. Attorney and insurance company director Elizabeth De Villing tells of one. "I carry a soft briefcase with a shoulder strap. It looks sort of like a purse. You're not supposed to take briefcases into the Supreme Court Library, but you can take purses. When I go to the library, this briefcase becomes a purse." —*D.D.*

HEARD THE ONE ABOUT
THE TRAVELING BUSINESSWOMAN?

Interview by Patricia Skalka

It's a truism in our world that consultants and advisers will *always* find something to consult and give advice about.

In this decade, the prime candidate seems to be the emerging business-woman, the woman executive. A veritable stranger in a strange land, she needs—we are told—help in dressing, talking, acting, looking and feeling like a success. And she needs it most, says John T. Molloy, author of the best-selling *Dress For Success* (for men) and the recently-published *Women's Dress For Success Book,* when she travels.

The reason is obvious. Traveling is a relatively new game to women business executives. They can't draw on past experiences or the accumulated knowledge of other women. They encounter problems—*new* problems—and they need to learn how to cope with them.

The solution, says Molloy, a former teacher turned management consultant, is *image.* Image has sold presidential candidates, and it can sell executives, too—either male or female. The right image bestows both authority and power. And according to Molloy, who has spent 17 years collecting data on how clothes make the person, the woman who carries the right image on a business trip also takes with her the aura of authority and power. *Ipso facto,* she has a better chance of being treated like the executive she is..

Following the publication of his first book, Molloy was dubbed "America's first wardrobe engineer" by *Time* Magazine. Since then, he's become a $1500-a-day consultant to many of America's leading corporations.

TWA Ambassador asked Molloy to elaborate on the problems of the traveling businesswoman. To interview him, we dispatched Patricia Skalka, a busy freelance writer, former editor and frequent traveler. Here's her report:

"Molloy's information comes from the research that went into his two books and from a backup advisory group of 100 executive women. Whatever the question, he always comes back to image. His solutions are absolute, rigid, confining. Individuality flies out the door in the face of statistics. He dismisses disagreement: you are wrong, the statistics are right. The gospel according to John Molloy: don't do what you like or enjoy, do what tests best. And he delivers the message authoritatively.

"John Molloy is not concerned with change. His context is what exists now—prejudices, conditioning, conservatism, no matter how illogical or unfair. The underlying argument is simple: men have had to play by these rules, and now—like it or not—women have to play by them, too. Either that or go back to their kitchens.

"But Molloy takes the businesswoman seriously. This alone is beneficial. Whether she agrees or disagrees with his comments, his data, his pronouncements, the businesswoman is *forced* to take a second or third look at how she handles herself, how she copes—and she can't help but make that a hard and serious look."

TWA: Can you measure the effect traveling has on a woman's career and whether this is positive or negative?

Molloy: Travel impacts a woman's career more than a man's and impacts it negatively—at least up until now. We've found that women who traveled generally didn't succeed as well as women who didn't travel as part of their jobs. The reason is that the traveling woman didn't know how to take her power with her. It wasn't that she didn't know how to use power —women can use power. But they have to learn to take it with them.

TWA: What do you have to offer to make this power more profitable?

Molloy: Women need what I'm giving them and what corporate America recognizes—a "winner's work uniform." Not just a uniform that says "I'm working," but that "I'm working and I'm a winner." Men have a uniform like this. It's the male suit. Lots of people wear it who aren't winners, but that's beside the point—*all* winners wear it. It's an effective device. Women need a uniform, too. For them, it's the skirted suit.

All women have three basic problems, and the suit will help solve these. They have an authority problem—not because they're women, but because they're shorter, have smaller faces, smaller features. They have a problem with intentions. Many bosses still think women aren't committed to moving up. They have a problem with proving their competence. I can show up wearing a three-piece suit and people assume I'm competent until I stick my foot in my mouth. A woman shows up wearing just about anything and she has to continually prove her competence. Obviously, if we're equal, she is working under a disadvantage. The skirted suit, once it's recognized as the winner's work uniform, will solve these problems.

TWA: That sounds fine for the home office. But what if a woman doesn't *like* traveling in a skirted suit? What if she wants to wear pants for warmth and comfort?

Molloy: Tough. The successful woman *always, absolutely, positively* wears the skirted suit. Any woman who travels in anything else is an idiot. Look at me. You think I like wearing this suit? Ask 50 men if they like wearing suits—they'll all say no. But it's part of the uniform.

SHE FORGOT HER FEDORA
AND LOST THE ACCOUNT

TWA: Isn't that a step backward, a reversal of modern trends away from formal rigidity and dress codes? Why impose a uniform on women when, for the last decade, we've seen a trend away from this for men?

Molloy: No you haven't. I was at a steel company meeting where a young man asked me just the same thing. The vice president at the meeting said I didn't have to answer the question. He said the explosion of color and pattern in that company had been only in the mail room.

Okay, this may not be true in every company, but it is in the majority of companies and industries. Generally, there's been no dramatic shift in standards. And even if the men do shift, women should fight it because relaxing of standards puts them at a bigger disadvantage.

TWA: It would seem to open the door for more individuality and expression—why do you say it puts them at a disadvantage?

Molloy: We did research that showed women in the sun-belt, leisure environments and southern California tested more poorly than men. They were less authoritative. Men overshadowed women tremendously.

In the traditional strict environment—the Boston-banking, dark-suit, conservative kind of world—women were at an advantage to the point where strong women overshadowed weak men. I'm not sure of all the reasons, but I think part of it involves the "non-verbal communicants"—the clothes, the appearance. And all the studies on verbal and nonverbal communicants show the nonverbal are stronger. Women in these areas tended to adopt the conservative look and assumed part of the authority that goes with it.

TWA: How is this rigidity, this conservatism, going to help make traveling easier and more effective for busineswomen?

Molloy: Traveling women have three basic complaints. They are not treated well by service people—and this is partially their own fault because research shows they tip less than men. They have problems with how their co-workers react on meeting them. And they have problems with dining alone—getting poor service or lousy tables.

The business uniform will solve many of these problems. It tells service people you're important and will tip—and women should *always* tip well in uniform. The uniform tells the co-workers who stands where. The traveling woman doesn't have to explain her authority. Her clothes do it for her. She won't get a lousy table, either, or have to eat alone in her room, or have to put up with needless attention.

TWA: Can you describe two or three acceptable outfits the business-woman can use for traveling? Outfits that would produce these results?

Molloy: No, I can't. There *aren't* two outfits. Or three outfits. There is only one—the skirted suit. Here are the rules. The suit with a look of linen—and by suit I mean matching jacket and shirt. The skirt, two inches below the knee—that will get you by in New York and Kansas City both. The blouse, cotton and polyester.

If you're meeting a woman, wear a beige suit: if you're meeting a man, wear a darker gray suit; if you don't know, wear a lighter gray or tweed, but no tweed in the Northeast. Brown is fine anywhere from Ohio to Seattle—that's the brown belt. No vests—sexy. No pants, no dangling earrings. No boots—if you *have* to wear them, remove them before you arrive.

Simple pumps, plain stockings. Hair length, shoulder or shorter, nothing masculine. Makeup, minimal. Perfume, very expensive and very light. A wedding ring is terrific. I think women should wear one even if they're not married. It says you're reliable and conservative—even if you're not. And a hat—women should always wear a hat, the feminine fedora, everywhere. It works.

TWA: What if a woman looks terrible in a hat or hates wearing them?

Molloy: Tough. She wears one anyway. What if a man looks terrible in a suit? I still tell him to wear it.

TWA: You talk as if this is all some kind of game.

Molloy: It is. And this is for people who want to *play* the game. It's the dummies who don't even know there's a game going on who are in trouble. I'm not concerned about the person who doesn't care about the game. I'm doing this for people who want to win. Women don't know the game yet; they're just learning it. And they always ask the same question: shouldn't we loosen things up for everyone?

That's not the question. The question is: what do I do today to get bigger money and more power tomorrow? The only way women are going to loosen things up is by getting in. And women who get in don't want it loosened up because they recognize they're more effective when it isn't loosened up. I'll make a prediction: in 20 years, women are going to be the ones in industry who insist on keeping the dress code because it's to their advantage to do so. And I can see women quitting companies that loosen up dress codes, as a threat to their careers.

TWA: Are you serious?

Molloy: No question at all.

TWA: You're talking specifically about clothes and how they contribute to image. There must be other travel props that you've found effective.

Molloy: A man does all right with one old leather bag and another leather bag. But women test better with sets of luggage, and the sets that test best are canvas with leather belting and trim. Always carry an attache case—and make sure it matches the leather on the luggage. Service people look very closely at this. And insure your luggage. Women have a habit of walking into a hotel and standing by their bags. They guard their luggage. Don't do it. Put it down and walk up to the desk.

Women should always stay in better hotels. They should travel first-class when possible. *Never* take the bus. Take the metro only if it's convenient. Women who travel and sell by auto should drive smaller cars. The Mercedes works well, or the small Cadillac. Always reserve a high-priced, full sedan. And be specific. If you ask for a certain kind of car, they'll get it for you.

Avoid nice little wash-and-wear items—they never wash and wear. Send clothes out for dry cleaning. Use a corporate identification when you call and reserve a table: say, "This is Ms. Thomas from Blue Box." And always use a business card as the ID on your attache case. Never anything else. Avoid umbrellas if you can. And never carry anything that is too heavy for you. You shouldn't come off the plane lugging a bag you can't handle. Check the bag and get one with a set of wheels. Nothing makes a woman look more inefficient than carrying something that is too heavy.

Women who have glasses should always wear them traveling. It adds weight to the face, makes them look like they have more authority. The watch should be plain with Roman numerals, and the pen gold, not silver. And never bring a yellow pad into a meeting. If you're going to take notes, use a white pad.

I don't know if a woman traveling alone should have a drink on a plane. **But if she is with a man, she should not drink, even if he does. Although I've** had some women tell me that it's different if you're in First Class and something is given to you.

The attache case is a must—get one with a purse built into it, but never carry a purse *and* an attache case. If you can, pack perfumes and things in your luggage; if they're in your case, secure them. One woman told me how she got up to make a presentation, opened her attache case, and watched as her perfume and makeup spilled out on the desk. It killed her.

TWA: Are businesswomen more at an advantage or disadvantage when traveling alone or with a co-worker?

Molloy: That I don't really know. However, if a woman is traveling with a male assistant, she should always initiate the conversation when they arrive, introducing him as "my assistant Mr. X." This clearly establishes relationships right from the start. If she is traveling with a male who is her equal, then she should dress as conservatively as he—she *has* to, just to survive. And when she is traveling with another woman of different rank, they should recognize their different relative positions and dress accordingly. The one in charge wears a darker suit—then they don't have to start explaining who's who. They're ready to work together as a team to get the job done.

TWA: All this concern for detail—gold pen versus silver pen, and so on. Is there a logical explanation for preference other than "it tests better"?

Molloy: There is probably a logical explanation for everything here. But nobody wants to pay for research to uncover the explanation. They just want to know what works best. Let me give you a further example of how this can be broken down. Let's take a woman and prescribe the color of her suit on the basis of whom she is going to be meeting with.

For example: a woman accountant meeting other accountants wears a blue suit. A woman accountant meeting a client wears a gray suit. A woman in sales dresses to sell the product, not to look *chic*. We found that women in the drug industry got into the doctors' offices more quickly if they were dressed more *chicly*—and they tested about the same with men on selling traditional medications, but they had better records with new drugs if they were dressed more conservatively. All we know is what works.

TWA: What about pitfalls? Where is the traveling woman the weakest?

Molloy: Resort training conferences are the death knell for women. Men already have a uniform for these occasions—it's the shirt with the little alligator. But women make two basic mistakes: they continue to wear their suits, which puts them out of place, or they go and look all feminine.

They should wear traditional, conservative, upper-middle-class sports wear. Pants are okay, but no sweaters, no sandals, no jeans—even if they're *chic*. Avoid the pool, discourage the beach buffet, and stay away from sport competitions, even if you're very good.

TWA: That's hardly fair and equal treatment.

Molloy: Nobody says it is. Men can still work up what's called a sweat. When women get disheveled they start losing authority. Men don't, not completely, and I don't know why. By the way, the advice I give women —I realize it isn't great.

TWA: As a result of all this, then, you have people—in this case, women —getting in on *image,* not on ability.

Molloy: Oh, no. That's not true. Image won't get you in. *But lack of image will keep you out.* There's always the exception. I'm talking about 99.9 per cent. There's Barbara Walters—but she's an actress. A good one, but an actress. People point to Mary Wells. She's *chic*, but she's selling a different product. I'm sure she's a very successful businesswoman, but she's not typical.

TWA: You do allow for exceptions, even to your rules?

Molloy: There are exceptions all the time. But what I'm doing is giving women the house odds. Giving them a batting-average percentage. It's a very simple formula. It's clean and it works every time. I give women this counsel—don't take 85 per cent of this advice, take all of it or forget it. Don't think you're the one who can carry off the exception.

TWA: Surely attitude must play a role, at home and while traveling. What about the *you,* the person behind the image?

Molloy: Women should adopt a businesslike attitude—what that is I can't define, and I'm not going to give an opinion.

TWA: But if you don't have a positive attitude, an attitude that says "I'm sure of myself"—then you won't step ahead and introduce your business cohort as your assistant. You won't do the things you're telling women to do.

Molloy: Oh no. Wait a second. Let me tell you about some studies we did with people who were rather sick and had personality problems. I'm not implying that women have personality problems. I worked in conjunction with several psychologists counseling patients who had problems dealing with the world. We found that by picking their clothing we changed how the world dealt with them, and therefore changed their attitude toward the world.

A good part of the attitude problem for women will be solved by the uniform. If people start treating a woman like an authority figure, she's going to start acting like one. One of the reasons women don't act like an authority is because no one treats them like one. It's a constant fight. But I'm going to give them something that will take the burden off their shoulders so they don't have to fight every five minutes before people will accept them. And it's going to succeed. It's going to work, and it's catching on.

Three years from now, 50 per cent of women executives traveling on planes will be wearing skirted suits. You'll be able to tell winners and losers as they walk down the ramp.

TWA: It seems ironic that on the one hand women have broken old bonds, and now you've got this movement going to put them in new bonds.

Molloy: Women happen to need more status symbols than men. Always? Probably not. But right now they do. I am interested in *now*. I'm not saying any of this is fair. I'm not saying this is the way it should be. But this is the way it *is*. And most women I interview who are in business say, "Yes, you're right—unfortunately."

I thought I would get a much different reaction. I thought I would get a violent, negative reaction from women themselves. The only people I hear from are in the fashion industry, and I could care less. The women in business have been surprisingly positive to me. They argue a little, but at the end of the argument they say I'm right.

TWA: There are many women, and others, who will disagree with you and claim you're taking something away from women—a freedom, an independence. What would you say to them?

Molloy: Only that the people who give them this freedom are keeping them in the typing pool. I am not liberating women.   I am restricting them —I'm putting them under *tremendous* restrictions. I understand the advice is not pleasant, but I'm going to get them out of the secretarial pools. If they do exactly as they're told—exactly as the research dictates —they will absolutely succeed. It works.

If a woman reads this and disagrees, she shouldn't write a letter immediately. I challenge her to try it for one month, try it on her next three trips, and *then* see what happens. Then see what kind of letter she'll write.

TWA Ambassador, February 1978

PROFESSIONAL DEVELOPMENT

Reference List

INTRODUCTION TO THE HOME ECONOMICS PROFESSION

Bonde, Ruth L. A Time of Growth, A Time of Decisions. *Journal of Home Economics,* Vol. 68, No. 1, January 1976, pp. 29-31.

Hastrop, Kathleen. "Bridging the Gap—The Role of the Professional Home Economist." *Journal of Consumer Studies and Home Economics,* Vol. 1, No. 2 (June 1977), pp. 93-100.

Home Economics: New Directions II. *Journal of Home Economics,* Vol. 67, No. 3, May 1975, pp. 26-28.

Marshall, William H. Issues Affecting the Future of Home Economics. *Journal of Home Economics,* Vol. 65, No. 6, September 1973, pp. 8-10.

McFarland, Keith. The Home Economics Image Study—What We Learned and Did Not Learn—What We Need To Know. (Speech presented at the annual meeting of The American Home Economics Association, June 25, 1975, San Antonio, Texas.)

Spitze, H.T. Home Economics in the Future, *Journal of Home Economics*, Vol. 68, No. 4, September 1976, pp. 5-8.

Weis, Susan, M. East and S. Manning. Home Economics Units in Higher Education: A Decade of Change, *Journal of Home Economics,* Vol. 66, No. 5, May 1974, pp. 11-15.

Daniel Yankelovich, Inc., Home Economist Image Study, A Qualitative Investigation, Prepared for American Home Economics Association, May 1974.

PERSONAL QUALITIES OF THE PROFESSIONAL— EFFECTIVENESS AT WORK

Alberti, Robert E. and Emmons, Michael L. *Stand Up, Speak Out, Talk Back*. Paperback, 1975.

*Alberti, Robert E. and Emmons, Michael L. *Your Perfect Right: A Guide to Assertive Behavior*. San Luis Obispo, Calif.: Impact, 1974.

Bloom, Lynn, A., Coburn, Karen and Pearlman, Joan. *New Assertive Woman*. New York: Delacorte Press, 1975.

The Creative Woman. U.S. Government Printing Office, Washington, D.C.

Curley, Jayme. *The Balancing Act*. Chicago: Chicago Review Press/Swallow Press, 1976.

Davis, Keith, *Human Behavior at Work, Human Relations and Organizational Behavior*, McGraw Hill, Inc., 1972, pp. 234-250.

Fensterstein, Herbert and Baer, Jean. *Don't Say Yes When You Want to Say No*. New York: Dell Publishing Co. 1975.

Jakubowski-Spector, P. Facilitating the Growth of Women Through Assertive Training, *The Counseling Psychologist*, Vol. 4 (1973), pp. 75-86.

Kanter, Rosabeth Moss. The Impact of Hierarchical Structures on the Work Behavior of Women and Men, *Social Problems*, Vol. 23/24 (April 1976).

Maineri, Sandra C. Creating a Career: How I Developed a Job Market as a Free-Lance Home Economist. *Journal of Home Economics*, Vol. 68, No. 4 (September 1976).

Phelps, Stanley and Austin, Nancy. *The Assertive Woman*. San Luis Obispo, Calif.: Impact, 1975.

Rathus, S.A. An Experimental Investigation of Assertive Training in a Group Setting, *Journal of Behavior Therapy and Experimental Psychiatry*, Vol. 3 (1972), pp. 81-86.

Rathus, S.A. Instigation of Assertive Behavior Through Videotape—Mediated Assertive Model and Directed Practice. *Behavior Research and Therapy*, Vol. II, No. 1, February 1973, pp. 57-65.

Rosen, Benson and Thomas H. Jordee. *Becoming Aware*. Science Research Associates: Chicago, 1976.

Smith, Manuel J. *When I Say No, I Feel Guilty*. New York: The Dial Press, 1975.

U.S. Department of Labor, Employment Standards Administration, Women's Bureau, *A Working Woman's Guide to Her Job Rights*, Washington, D.C.: U.S. Government Printing Office, Superintendent of Documents. 1975.

U.S. Department of Labor, Employment and Training Administration. *Women and Work*, U.S. Government Printing Office, Washington, D.C., 1977. 1977.

Entire Issue of *Journal of Home Economics*, Vol. 67, No. 4, July 1975.

ENTERING THE PROFESSION: RESUME, INTERVIEWING, LETTER WRITING

Bolles, Richard N. *What Color is Your Parachute?* Berkeley, California: Ten Speed Press, 1975.

Bostwick, Burdette E. *Resume Writing: A Comprehensive How-To-Do-It Guide*. John Wiley and Sons, New York, 1976.

Brennan, Lawrence D., Strand, Stanley, and Gruber, Edward C. *Resumes for Better Jobs,* New York: Simon and Schuster, 1973.

Donaho, Melvin W. and Hohn L. Meyer. *How to Get the Job You Want.* Prentice Hall, Inc., Englewood Cliffs, N.J., 1967.

Dunphy, Philip W., Austin, Sidney F. and McEneaney, Thomas J., *Career Development for the College Student.* Cranston, R.I.: The Carroll Press, 1973.

Dynamics of Job Interviewing—The Face to Face Encounter. Symbiotic Learning Systems, 1977 (audio cassette).

Endicott, Frank S. *A College Student's Guide to Career Planning.* Rand McNally and Company, 1967.

German, Donald R. and Joan W. German. *Successful Job Hunting for Executives.* Chicago, Illinois: Henry Regnery Co., 1974.

Irish, R.K. *Go Hire Yourself an Employer.* Garden City, New York: Doubleday, 1973.

Kelley, E. *et al.,* How to Help Your Students be Successful at Job Hunting, *Journal of Home Economics,* Vol. 68, No. 4 (November 1976), pp. 32-35.

Lewis, Adele. *How to Write Better Resumes.* Woodbury, New York: Barron's, 1977.

Nutter, Carolyn F. *The Resume Workbook.* Craston, Rhode Island: Carroll Press, 1970.

Pletcher, Barbara A. *Saleswoman: A Guide to Career Success.* Dow-Jones-Irwin, Homewood, Illinois, 1978.

Powell, C.R. *Career Planning and Placement for the College Graduate of the 1970's.* Dubuque, Iowa: Kendall/Hunt Publishing Co., 1974.

Resume Preparation Manual: A Step-by-Step Guide, Catalyst, 1976.

RESEARCH IN HOME ECONOMICS

Kies, Constance, How One Researcher Copes with Controversy, *Journal of Home Economics,* Vol. 65, No. 1, January 1973, pp. 35-36.

Montgomery, James E. and S.J. Ritchey. Home Economics Research: Are We Doing All We Can? *Journal of Home Economics,* Vol. 67, No. 1, January 1975, pp. 35-39.

Refer to *Home Economics Research Journal* for an overview of research in Home Economics.

LIFE-LONG LEARNING — GRADUATE SCHOOL AND CONTINUING EDUCATION

Gnagey, Theodore P. "Education is Life." I, II *Adult Leadership,* XX Nos. 5 & 6, Nov-Dec 1971, pp. 179-181 FF. and 217-219.

Newkirk, Gwendolyn. Women in the Future. *Journal of Home Economics,* Vol. 68, No. 4 (September 1976), pp. 12-14.

Perry, Margaret and Lura M. Odlund. An Interdisciplinary Doctoral Program in Home Economics. *Journal of Home Economics,* Vol. 68, No. 5 (November 1976), pp. 24-28.

Snow, Phyllis. An Interstate Doctoral Program in Home Economics. *Journal of Home Economics,* Vol. 68, No. 5 (November 1976), pp. 24-28.

LEGISLATIVE PROCESS

Jolley, Mary Allen. Some Myths About Legislative Action, *Journal of Home*

Economics, Vol. 66, No. 1, January 1974, pp. 13-16. See complete issue, if possible.

Ruffing, Susan. *The Legislative Process.* Ohio State University Telecommunications, 1977. (video cassette)

Ruffing, Susan. *The Home Economist in Public Affairs,* Ohio Home Economics Association, Ohio State University Telecommunications, 1978. (video cassette)

PUTTING IT TOGETHER: PROFESSIONAL AAA

Molloy, John T. *The Woman's Dress for Success Book.* Chicago: Follett Publishing Co. 1977.

Molloy, John T. *Dress for Success.* New York: Peter H. Wyden/Publisher. 1975.

STANDING UP FOR YOU

References

Alberti, R.E. and Emmons, M.L., *Stand Up, Speak Out, Talk Back!* New York: Pocket Books, Inc., 1975.

Bandura, A., "Analysis of Modeling Processes." In A. Bandura (Ed.), *Psychological Modeling.* Chicago: Aldine Ahterton, 1971.

Bates, H.D. and Zimmerman, S.F., "Toward the Development of a Screening Scale for Assertion Training." *Psychological Reports,* 28 (1971), pp. 99-107.

Ellis, A., *Reason and Emotion in Psychotherapy.* New York: Lyle Stuart, 1962.

Fensterheim, H. and Baer, J., *Don't Say Yes When You Want To Say No.* New York: Dell Publishing Company, Inc., 1975.

Galassi, J.P., DeLo, J.S., Gallasi, M.D. and Bastien, S., "The College Self-Expression Scale: A measure of assertiveness." *Behavior Therapy,* (1974), pp. 165-171.

Hoffman, B., *The Relative Effectiveness of Three Types of Group Assertive Training.* Unpublished doctoral dissertation, The University of Texas at Austin, 1974.

Jakubowski-Spector, P., "Assertive Training for Women." Colloquium presented at Southern Illinois University, Carbondale, Illinois, 1973.

Jakubowski-Spector, P., "Facilitating the Growth of Women Through Assertive Training." *The Counseling Psychologist,* 4 (1973), pp. 75-86.

Kagen, N., *Interpersonal Process Recall: a method of influencing human interaction.* East Lansing: Michigan State University, 1975.

Lamb, K., *Self-Directed Relaxation: a self-serving smorgasbord.* Unpublished manuscript, The Ohio State University, 1976.

McFall, R.M. and Maraston, A.R., "An Experimental Investigation of Behavior and Rehearsal in Assertive Training." *Journal of Abnormal Psychology,* 76 (1970), pp. 295-303.

Osborn, S. and Harris, G. *Assertive Training for Women.* Springfield, Ill.: Charles C. Thomas Publisher, 1975.

Phelps, S. and Austin, N., *The Assertive Woman.* Fredericksburg, Va.: Impact, 1975.

Weigel, R.G., *Developing Individual Behavioral Change Goals.* Unpublished manuscript, Colorado State University, 1972.

Weiskott, G., *Assertiveness, Territoriality, and Personal Space as a Function of Group Assertion Training with a College Population.* Unpublished doctoral disseration, The University of Texas at Austin, 1975.

Wolpe, J. "The Instigation of Assertive Behavior: Transcript from Two Cases." *Journal of Behavior Therapy and Experimental Psychiatry,* 1 (1970) pp. 145-151.

Bibliography for Text

*Alberti, R.E. and Emmons, M.L., *Your Perfect Right.* San Luis Obispo: Impact, 1970.

Angel, Juvenal L. *Specialized Resumes for Executives and Professionals.* New York: Regents Publishing, 1967.

Association of American Publishers. *Copyright Permissions: A Guide for Non Commercial Use.*

Association of American Publishers. *Explaining the New Copyright Law.*

*Bandura, A., *Principles of Behavior Modification.* New York: Holt, Rinehart & Winston, 1969.

*Bloom, L., Coburn, K. and Pearlman, J., *The New Assertive Woman.* New York: Delacorte Press, 1975.

Bostwick, Burdette. *Resume Writing: A Comprehensive How-to-Do-It Guide.* New York: John Wiley & Sons, 1976.

Brecker and Merryman, Inc. *How to Get a Job.* Armco Steel Corporation.

Carney, Clarke; Streufert, Don; Field, Cinda. *Career Planning.* The Ohio State University Counseling and Consultation Service, 1977.

*Chickering, A.W., *Education and Identity.* San Francisco: Jossey-Bass, 1969.

Coppola, Nancy W. "The Woman in the Gray Flannel Suit." Reprinted from the February 1977 issue of *Boston Magazine* in *Eastern Airlines Review,* October 1977, pp. 34-38, 82.

Donaho, Melvin and Meyer, John. *How to Get the Job You Want.* Englewood Cliffs, New Jersey: Prentice-Hall, Inc., 1976.

Gunther, Max. "How to Make a Good First Impression." *Family Circle.* August 7, 1978, pp. 36-38, 66, 166.

Glass, Elwood, Jr. *Job Offer Comparator.* Standard Oil Company of Ohio.

Huseman, Richard; Logue, Al; Freshley, D. *Readings in Interpersonal and Organizational Communication.* Boston: Holbrook Press, 1969.

Hogan, Betsy. "How to Get Hired for More Money." Reprint from April 1978 *Redbook.*

How to Get a Job: It's Your Move. The Ohio Bureau of Employment Services.

Irish, Richard K. Go Hire Yourself an Employer. Garden City, New York: Anchor Press/Doubleday, 1973.

*Jakubowski-Spector, P., *Assertive Training for Women Part I and Part II.* Washington, D.C.: American Personnel and Guidance Association Films, 1972.

*Lange, A. and Jakubowski, P., *Responsible Assertive Behavior: Cognitive-behavioral procedures for trainers.* Champaign-Urbana, Ill.: Research Press, 1976.

*Lazarus, A.A., *Behavior Therapy and Beyond.* New York: McGraw-Hill, 1971.

Loevy, Diana. "The Image Makers." *Audio-Visual Communications,* May 1978.

*MacNeilage, L., *Assertion Training Guidelines.* Unpublished manuscript, The University of Texas at Austin, 1972.

*McFall, R.M. and Lillesand, D.B., "Behavioral Rehearsal with Modeling and Coaching in Assertion Training." *Journal of Abnormal Psychology,* 77 (1971), pp. 313-323.

Molloy, John. *The Women's Dress For Success Book.* Chicago: Follett, 1977.

Office Dress Counts. Pentagon I Chapter of Federally Employed Women, Inc., 1976.

*Rathus, S.A., "An Experimental Investigation of Assertive Training in a Group Setting." *Journal of Behavior Therapy and Experimental Psychiatry,* 3 (1972) pp. 81-86.

Skalka, Patricia. "Heard the One About the Traveling Businesswoman?" *TWA Ambassador,* February 1978, pp 18-21, 42.

*Smith, M.J., *When I Say No, I Feel Guilty.* New York: Dial Press, 1975.

Sommer, Dale W. "How Clothes Shape Your Future." *Industry Week,* October 10, 1977, pp. 52-56.

The State Library Review. A Report from the State Library of Ohio, 1976-1977.

Stevenson, Gloria. *Beginner's Guide to Work.* Ohio Bureau of Employment Services.

Tittle, Diana. "How Women Can Dress for Success." *Cleveland Magazine,* May 1977, pp. 86-90.

*Weiskott, G. and Sparks, M., "Assertion Training: Non-Verbal Components." In Pfeiffer and Jones, *Structured Experiences, Volume VI.* LaJolla: University Associates, 1977 (in press).

"What Teachers and Libraries Can and Can't Do Under the New Law." *The Chronicle of Higher Education,* October 11, 1976, XIV, 6, p. 1.

*Wolpe, J., *The Practice of Behavior Therapy.* New York: Pergamon Press, 1969.

*Wolpe, J. and Lazarus, A.A., *Behavior Therapy Techniques.* Oxford: Pergamon Press, 1966.

WOSU Broadcast, Access Continuing Education, January 6, 1978. Speakers were Dr. Robeson, Tom Lisk, and Dorothy Geiger.

You and Your Government: Suggestions for Effective Advocacy for Ohio's Older Americans. Ohio Commission on Aging, December 1975.

*These materials were used as references in the preparation of the section— "Standing Up For YOU " for this manual.